TIME GENIUS

DESIGN, ACHIEVE, AND IMPLEMENT ANY GOAL INTO YOUR ALREADY HECTIC, CRAZY LIFE (OR BUSINESS)

Chris Griffin

Glazer-Kennedy
publishing

An imprint of Morgan James Publishing

Time Genius

Design, Achieve, and Implement Any Goal Into Your
Already Hectic, Crazy Life (or Business)

ISBN 978-0-98237-937-0

Library of Congress Control Number: 2010920811

Glazer-Kennedy
publishing

An imprint of
Morgan James Publishing
1225 Franklin Ave., STE 325
Garden City, NY 11530-1693
Toll Free 800-485-4943
www.MorganJamesPublishing.com

In an effort to support local communities, raise awareness and funds, Morgan James Publishing donates one percent of all book sales for the life of each book to Habitat for Humanity. Get involved today, visit www.HelpHabitatForHumanity.org.

Table of Contents

Preface. 1

Section I

Chapter 1 7
Understanding the 12 Laws of Time
Twelve Laws from the 4th Dimension
      The Laws of Time Cycle   15

Chapter 2 19
STOP! (Time) Thief
They do walk among us.

Chapter 3 29
From Prussia with Love
The Most Efficient War Ever

Section II

Chapter 1 39
Law 1: Goals
Goals Are Worthless …

Chapter 2 49
Law 2: Right Mind
Use your head for something besides a hat rack.

Chapter 3 57
Law 3: Belief
Go Tell it on the Mountain

Chapter 4 67
Law 4: Courage
You've got to fight for your right.

Chapter 5 77
Law 5: Visual Learning
The Show Me State of Mind

Chapter 6 85
Law 6: Operations
"What are we talking about … practice?"

Chapter 7 95
Law 7: Logistics
Your Own Personal Traffic Controller

Chapter 8 105
Law 8: Environment
God Save the Environment!

Chapter 9 113
Law 9: Standard Operating Procedures
Keeping the Dark Ages at Bay

Chapter 10 125
Law 10: Discipline
Keep It Together

Chapter 11 137
Law 11: Motivation
If you can't get excited about this …

Chapter 12 145
Law 12: The Golden Rule
All Hail the King

<u>Section III</u>
Workbook
    Law 1—Goals 156
    Law 2—Right Mind 158
    Law 3—Belief 159
    Law 4—Courage 160
    Law 5—Visual Learning 161
    Law 6—Operations 162

    Law 7—Logistics. 164
    Law 8—Environment 166
    Law 9—Standard Operating Procedures 167
    Law 10—Discipline 169
    Law 11—Motivation. 170
    Law 12—The Golden Rule 172

A-ha Moments 175

About the Author 177

Free Bonus Gift. 179

Preface

My name is Chris Griffin, and I am a dentist.

WARNING: The book you are about to read has lots of heavy psychological stuff in it. Let it be known that I am not a psychologist. I am not a psychiatrist. Heck, I didn't even stay in the right kind of hotel last night. What you will see are strong opinions that I hold. I believe they are absolutely true, but you have to be responsible enough to see if they will work the same way for you. Don't take my word for it; try it yourself and see. Then, when you have a major breakthrough and want to tell me how that feels, e-mail me at Chris@3daydentist.com and tell me about it.

Now that that's out of the way, why should you listen to me? Well, let me give you a little background on myself and let you decide if I am someone whose opinion might give you some benefit. Before you start reading this book, I think it would be a good idea to give y'all an idea of where I am coming from and how all this got started.

First off, notice I used the word *y'all*. I know that's not proper English, but I'm from the South and that's definitely proper Southern English. I am from Mississippi. We are *always* ranked dead last in every category you might see states ranked for "good" things. You might see us ranked close to first if someone is ranking "bad" things, like poverty, unemployment, welfare recipients, etc. I always knew it would be hard making a living here, but I came home anyway. I have lots of relatives who fled this place for greener pastures up North (Virginia and Maryland are definitely North for someone from Mississippi) and have done well, but I guess I am just an old softy for the memories I have from my childhood.

I was valedictorian of my high school and had lots of options for college, but once again I couldn't bring myself to get too far from home and proudly went to Mississippi State University. No, not Ole Miss. Down here in the Southeastern Conference, it is a *big* mistake calling one college by their rival's name. So please don't ask me at a seminar how the Rebels are doing. I am a Bulldog deep down and have suffered through many sports seasons for it.

One of the dreams I always had as a kid was to be a public speaker. I had gone with my family to see a concert by a famous Mississippian and fellow alumnus of Mississippi State, comedian Jerry Clower. He had made the audience feel so alive and special that night, I knew that I wanted to do that, too. A few years ago, I put myself through the laws in this book with the Definite Ideal Goal that I wanted to be able to speak to large crowds. Public speaking has always been hard for me. The first time I had to try it was giving the valedictory address at my eighth-grade graduation. I found that I couldn't breathe and barely got through a poem by Robert Frost without passing out. Somehow I squeaked through it. It has gotten better every time I go out there, but I'm still not the best. So please cut me some slack on the presentation the next time you hear me, because I promise I have put my blood, sweat, and tears into developing the content. Still, know that when I get up and speak in front of hundreds of people, it is a truly remarkable improvement and one that I don't think would be possible without following the truth in these laws.

It became evident that my associateship wasn't going to work out and I was going to have to find another way to support my family besides working for my childhood dentist. I found myself without a job, without any prospect of a job in a fifty-mile radius, and with a wife four months pregnant with my first child, and with *lots* of debt from school.

At first, I tried to get a job as an associate in the surrounding area. When that fell through, I was unsure of the right direction. I had always kind of breezed through life. I had played more golf in college than I should have. I had good intentions when I started out in engineering school, but when I discovered how hard engineer's work and how little they get paid commensurately, I knew I had to find another major. When my childhood dentist suggested dentistry, I figured that was for me. So I switched majors to something super easy, biological sciences. I got into dental school after three years at State and went to dental school in Memphis. I am sorry to say that I didn't take that too seriously either. When I should have been busting my butt to be the best possible, I was slipping out of class to surf the Internet or read the sports page. Let me insert here that even though I was a big-time slacker in dental school, I did earn the nickname "spring butt." I still haven't gotten an exact definition out of my friends as to why they called me that. I'll venture a guess that it had something to do with my study habits. As I said, I would goof off most of the semester until it was crunch time. Then, miraculously, with a little aid from late-night combos of sweet tea and coffee, I would spring into action. I have always had the ability to zero in on any target I wanted to hit, like a midterm test or the like. I could usually make up for weeks of non-study by blazing through hundreds of pages in the book in one night. Then, on test day, I would be jumpy and energetic, much to the aggravation of my close group of friends. Sometimes they outscored me, sometimes I outscored them, but I will guarantee that I put in less study time per course than anyone in my class. Somehow I made it through dental school ranked somewhere in the middle of the pack, and I went right into this sweet little associateship. So far in life, I hadn't really been challenged and I hadn't risked very much. Boy, was that about to change.

The associateship didn't work out. I was feeling like a ship in the doldrums. My mind was aimlessly drifting around with no direction and no hope of trade winds from the distance to help. When you are confronted with a crossroads in life, you always have some choices. Up till then, you would have been hard-pressed to call me anything but lazy. But sitting on my kitchen floor in June of 1999, something clicked deep inside of me. It was my very first a-ha moment. I firmly fixed the goal in my mind that I was going to build an amazing dental practice from scratch, right in my hometown. I knew that my conscience wouldn't abide failure. There was also no safe route for me to take this time. I had to zero in on my goal and be courageous if this was going to work out. The very next day, I got a call from a distant cousin of mine about an old house she knew about that might make a good dental office. It was in the heart of town on one acre of land. I closed on that property one week later. I found a retired carpenter to help me renovate it, and by June 15, we began the project. I worked day and night, every day, going on four hours of sleep or less. During the day, I helped the carpenter, and at night I cleaned up and did the projects that I was skilled enough to do. Throughout all this, I was interviewing and hiring and negotiating with a dental supply company. Mind you, I had no experience in any of this, but I had no choice. I had to get it done for my family and myself. I am proud to say that on August 30, 1999, I saw my first patient, and my grand opening was the next day. When the dust settled, I had managed to convert an old, run-down house into a three-operatory dental office, fully stocked and staffed, with completed grounds to boot. It had cost me a little less than $200,000 for *everything*. That had bought the land, the building, all the renovation, and equipment. Don't forget about all the inspections from the city and state that had to go on during that time.

I guess since I was used to working *that* hard, I went right on and worked *six* days a week for the first year or so.

My next goal was to cut back to three days a week and increase my income. At the time I might as well have been making the goal of becoming governor of the great state of Mississippi. It seemed improbable. I did the research and found someone who led me to believe that it was possible. Dr. Scott Perkins of Houston, Texas, is a man that I consider the grandfather of dental efficiency. He taught me that most of the time in a dentist's day is simply squandered. I drove to Houston a few times, and he taught me new ways to think about my business. I set a series of goals over the next few years and I have slowly knocked them out. I have been slowly whittling down the number of days I work ever since. Strangely enough, I have been fortunate enough to have an increase in my office production and collections every time I have cut down my working hours. The decrease in overall hours worked has also led me to need to maximize every second that I spend on patient care. I have become very stingy with my time overall, but especially with my time during patient care hours. I have dedicated myself to being the most effective I can be, every second of the workday, and through lots of trial and error (mostly error), I have come up with a new way of looking at things. Because of these new paradigms, we have found ourselves *slashing our procedure time in half, over and over again.* That has become the heartbeat of our office and the motivation to take this message on the road. As far as I know, this isn't even a statistic that is kept in my industry, but I'll just come right out and say that we perform more procedures per hour than just about any dentist in the country. At least, I haven't personally found one who does more volume for a single operator. In my other company, Chris Griffin's Capacity College, I teach every dentist to get the most out of their time at the office. I want them to experience the success that I *know* they can achieve. Then they can afford to spend the rest of their time at home. When I hold seminars at my office, I get real *wow* responses and testimonials. One of my students from Colorado even said that my course was the best thing he had ever done in his life. Now, I'm sure he meant that in the sense of his dental experiences, but he wasn't far off.

If he applied my philosophies to his practice and was able to take off an extra two days a week, it really would be the best thing he had ever done in his life.

In the midst of all the stuff I have done in my life, I have finally managed to find my own core beliefs. I love to teach people to find theirs. When they do this, it will open their eyes as to why some things work so well for others, while their "identical" attempts at the same goal fall short. You have to always come from a place that allows you to let your core beliefs shine through. Hopefully, you will find your core belief along the way. I also want you to use this book to hang a few trophies on the wall. Knock out some of those goals you have lying around the house and see what it does for your life. If you really focus and try your best, you will probably find yourself accomplishing so much more than your peers that it isn't even close. You will own the ability to command the most precious element in existence today. That's when you will earn the title, Time Genius.

Chapter 1

───────

Understanding the 12 Laws of Time
Twelve Laws from the 4th Dimension

That kind of sounds weird, but there is some significance in the association of time and the number twelve. There are twelve months in the year. There are two sets of twelve hours in a day, twelve hours for day and twelve hours for night. Twelve is divisible into the number of minutes in an hour and the number of seconds in a minute, sixty. It makes perfect since that there would be twelve laws in existence in the universe that time must obey to function. I believe that any person can harness the power of these twelve laws to turn that true currency of time into any material currency desired. Some people will turn time into money. Some will turn it into quality experience. Others will turn it into achievement. Whatever your wishes, you only have to learn the secrets of these laws and time can turn into anything your heart desires.

One of the greatest stumbling blocks to implementing your plan of action is to put off until another time the things that should be done right now. We cannot have indecision, because while we are thinking about doing something, we have already lost some of our precious time.

When Alexander the Great was asked how he had managed to conquer the world, he replied, "By not delaying." It is exactly the same with each of us. We are under the same laws of time that Alexander the Great had to obey. If we are to conquer the world, conquer ourselves, or solve a simple problem of management, we must act now and not delay. We must also follow our plan or system if we are to achieve our ideal goal.

After Alexander's death, Ptolemy continued his traditions in Alexandria, Egypt. There Euclid, the Father of Geometry, wrote the book *Elements,* the first work of geometry known to man.[1] The three dimensions we all can see and touch in this world belong to the 3-D Euclidian space. When time is added into the equation, you can see the progression of time when studying certain models. This study of time is referred to as the fourth dimension. Of course, mathematicians have greatly expanded on the ideas of Euclid, and a true mathematician or rocket scientist would cringe at my description. But hey, I took three years of physics in college, and by golly, I'm determined to use that knowledge for something before I die. The point is that although we have always understood that time obeyed certain laws and could be measured, studied, and predicted, we have rarely used this knowledge to our advantage in everyday modern life.

The better term for the universal rules presented in this book would probably be the Laws of Fourth-dimensional Euclidean Time or Minkowski Spacetime[2] for Practical Use During the Human Interaction on Planet Earth. You see why I have shortened the title of the concept to the Laws of Time.

WARNING: Do not read any further until you do this homework!

I thought I would throw out a little fun assignment for you before you get so deep into this book that you get lost. This manuscript

---

1   *http://en.wikipedia.org/wiki/Euclidean_geometry*
2   *http://en.wikipedia.org/wiki/Minkowski_space*

was meant to have the almost magical ability to assist a person in the achievement and implementation of any good, moral, and right-minded goal they could come up with. This could be as simple as learning how to run a new software program or as involved as becoming the president of the United States. I have no idea why anyone would want the latter job, but you could very well gain a position in life as impossibly fantastic as that by complete mastery of these twelve laws. The reason that most people sit around and make fun of the people who try to accomplish amazing things is that they have their own shortcomings in one of the twelve laws we will talk about. Just understanding that there are laws of the universe that you must obey and master to achieve something is a great step forward from the masses and puts you in the top tier of potential achievers. So, what is your first assignment?

To get you going down the right path, you must have a goal. Later, we will talk about forming your Definite Ideal Goal (DIG). That will be a very specific, detailed goal that you must clearly understand if you want to move forward. For now, you just need a vague understanding of something you want to accomplish, so that you can begin to form that DIG. This could be something that you know you want to accomplish but you just aren't clear on the details yet. Let me give you an example. Let's say that you are always having money troubles and that bothers you. Your vague goal—let's call it the Pre-Goal—is to make more money. Now, that is not very specific. You cannot move successfully through the twelve laws with that as your DIG and do any good. However, once that thought starts to percolate inside your mind as you continue to plod through this course, you will likely have an a-ha moment. That amazing gift from God will give you tremendous amounts of enthusiasm and power to define your DIG and move through this book.

Assignment #1: Define a Pre-Goal

What is some problem that you have? _____

_____

How does it make you feel?_____

_____

What is a way that you think you could solve it? _____

_____

Name the solution to the problem. _____

_____

How would solving the problem make you feel? _____

_____

Name the Pre-Goal. _____

_____

Now, go and answer the questions in the workbook section about the Pre-Goal.

The A-ha Moment

I don't know who first coined the phrase, but I certainly know one when I see one, and I have had a few in my lifetime. This is the Chris Griffin definition of an **a-ha moment:** *The moment in time in which a person fully grasps an idea, belief, or new concept with enough enthusiasm to move forward and take appropriate action. This moment can be coupled with periods of minutes, hours, or days of increased adrenaline and increased brain activity.* These moments are some of the best in our lives. I believe that the human brain has basically limitless power when it is firing on all cylinders, and these moments come as close as any I know of in tapping into that amazing energy we all have within ourselves.

We will need all that power and energy and more to withstand and win the battles that are sure to creep into our lives in the days immediately following our a-ha moment and any positive actions we take toward the concepts that led us there.

What battles am I talking about? There are battles with yourself, your staff, your spouse, and your friends. You have to win the battle with yourself first. If you don't believe you can do it, you have already lost. That is fixable if you really want to believe. If you can't make yourself believe in the new way at first, keep reading, studying, and visiting others who can do it. Associate with dentists who have already "made it." Before long, that battle will be behind you. What about the staff? Let me fill you in. They don't want to change. They will be perfectly content to rock along and remain at their current sickening level of average. They don't have to believe the same way you do (though it would be nice) but they do need to be properly motivated. Only you will be able to figure out the right incentives for yourselves or your staff. In my dental practice, we use team bonuses, individual bonuses, group bonuses, targeted bonuses, and whatever other bonus we can come up with to get our bunch happy about working toward our goals. I don't think there is ever a one-size-fits-all bonus for every situation. You will have to figure this one out. When you do, that battle is more than halfway won.

What's next? Ah yes, the spouse battle. Maybe your spouse is one of those types who gets behind you on every new idea you have. If so, great. Please skip to the next battle. Read on if your spouse needs a little encouragement to get on the bandwagon. Nothing can let the air out of your balloon as a motivated, believing, budding superstar implementer like a few negative words from the wife or husband. This is the one person in the world who can make you feel like a million bucks or a worthless scumbag. You really need your spouse behind you to make any serious changes in the way you do things. To do that, you will have to sell your idea to them. Don't announce that you are doing some new, scary thing. Slowly show them the new ways you have learned that will give you a better practice with more money, more time off, or more whatever (place benefit here). Some of them will take more convincing than others, but if you want to change, you have to stay the course.

Finally, the easiest battle, but not to be forgotten because of its subtle influence: your friends. You probably have friends who are at your same social or economic level. They are probably your friends because you all have lots of things in common. This means if you want to change yourself, you will be changing the dynamic relationship with those around you as well. If they are other people who are doing about as well as you, they won't want you to get better. If they are already the alpha dog in your peer group, they won't want someone else climbing up the ladder to claim "co-top dog" status. If they are other people who share your current enthusiasm about work, they won't really look forward to you suddenly loving your job and thus leaving their camaraderie group of being average. I'm certainly not saying that you should change friends, but just understand that some, if not all of them, will have varying degrees of non-support of your new lofty goals. Don't let their comments, overt or otherwise; sway you away from your new goals. Keep the faith.

As you read this book, you will experience several a-ha moments. I strongly encourage you to go to the end of the workbook, to the A-ha Moments pages and record them the second they come into your mind. Many times, clear, defined ideas become fuzzy and foggy with the passage of even a few seconds. Trust me. I have personal experience in this area. Remember, this book wasn't meant to be read straight through. Use it as a workbook and guide to help you implement your goal, then choose a new goal and do it again.

Sequential Cyclical Mind Maps

How can we harness the tremendous power contained in these laws? You could definitely use an outline. Most of my life, I have outlined my way to the attainment of goals. In the last ten years, I have found a way of literally mapping out my thoughts and projects. This new tool I use is called a mind map. These things have been around awhile and even were used way back in history by none other than Leonardo da Vinci. I have personally purchased a couple of mind-mapping software applications that I like. Mindmapper and Mindjet are both great programs. If you want to get in on the mind-mapping action without spending any extra money, you can find very adequate mind-mapping software at *http://www.bubble.us*, a free software site. After you navigate to this site, just click the big "Start Brainstorming" button and get started. Everything after that is pretty self-explanatory.

Resource Free Mind Mapping Software at *http://www.bubbl.us*

You can find more resources at www.timegeniusbook.com.

The reason I call the maps that you will create for this project "Sequential Cyclical Mind Maps" is that instead of having a central theme that all the Laws of Time will revolve around, each law should be taken in turn in the proper sequence. That is not to say that sometimes you will not need to pull some needed thoughts or actions from previous or future laws while you work your way through the current one. However, you need to finalize and seal each law before you move forward. Any unfinished business with any of the laws will come back to bite you as you move forward. They can also be cascading because, like I said, some values from each law may have to flow back or forward to help in the completion of any of the other laws. The way I represent this in my maps is to draw arrows from one law block to the one that needs the help to complete. When you are done, you have a large, orderly sequence with these little arrows flowing in every direction as the thoughts, actions, and values from any of the twelve laws may be needed in another law.

You can make mind maps for any of the any of your assignments as we move forward. You could make a giant one for the entire book if you desired. That one might be so huge that it would become cumbersome. I think a collection of smaller ones might do the best job, but make your own decision here. You can certainly write them out by hand, if that is the way that you think best. Da Vinci certainly drew some elegant ones without the aid of a supercomputer. Sometimes you just want to get away to think better. I know some people who are brilliant computer businessmen, who like to hike up into the mountains with only a backpack full of paper and pencils to hand draw mind maps for themselves and their companies. To each his own. You can always fall back on the old standby of the outline. I feasted on outlines throughout my entire run through high school, college, and graduate school. I'll even admit that I got the a-ha moment for this very book while I was sitting in the floor of my basement doing something else, and I grabbed the first pen and paper I could find to draw out the outline. It was only later that I refined my thoughts into a mind map. Certainly don't think that there is only one way to skin a cat.

Note: I would love to see some of the mind maps you have drawn to succeed in one of your goals due to this book. You can fax them to (662) 837-8199 or go to www.timegeniusbook.com.

P.P.S.

Perfectly Precise Summary
1.) Time is a precious physical commodity.
2.) Time must obey certain universal laws.
3.) You must define a "rough" Pre-Goal before you can define your real goal.
4.) Use a mind map or outline to get it down into a physical form.
5.) Don't waste your a-ha moments. Go straight to the a-ha page at the end of the book and write them down.

The Laws of Time Cycle

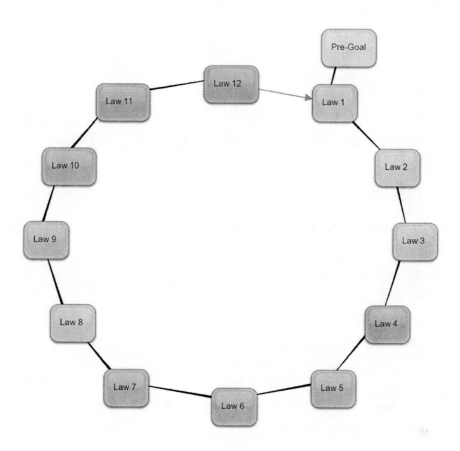

This kind of looks like a clock face, doesn't it? Don't think for a minute that is an accident. The laws of time revolve around the twelve laws, just like the time-measuring device is divided into twelve segments. It all flows this way very naturally. There are two kinds of laws here: thought laws and action laws. The thought laws are subdivided into two parts, too. These are Acquisition Thought Laws and Retention Thought Laws. You see, some necessary steps are held in the mind until they are completed. Then they spring into action with the Action Laws. Finally, more thought is required to maintain the achievement of the goal. I will list them below.

Acquisition Thought Laws:

1.) Goal
2.) Right Mind
3.) Belief
4.) Courage

Action Laws:

1.) Visual Learning – The bridge between thought and action
2.) Operations
3.) Logistics
4.) Environment
5.) Standard Operating Procedures

Retention Thought Laws:

1.) Discipline
2.) Motivation
3.) The Golden Rule

Of course, these can always interact with each other at any time, depending on the need of the person in pursuit of the goal. The sequence must be followed, but the individual laws can be called upon when need be.

The above image of a mind map from *www.bubbl.us* gives you the idea of the entire book. You enter the cycle at the Pre-Goal. You then jump right into the cycle and start out with Law 1, the Law of Goals. Here you will form your Definite Ideal Goal (DIG), and off you go. As you work through the problems associated with each of the laws and progress in the cycle, you come that much closer to attaining the DIG and implementing it. This book is not meant to be read straight through like a novel or everyday business book. This is a workbook throughout. Of course, there is a workbook section at the back, but you must keep up with the assignments as you go along. For example, you shouldn't read the chapter on Law 2 until you have finished the workbook portion for Law 1. That way, you will finish the book and workbook at just about the same time. Also, you will probably want to reuse this book over and over for different goal projects. If this is the case, you can always run off copies of the workbook section and keep the master pages in this book blank. Of course, you can always just buy a new book every time you want to start a new implantation project. Come to think of it, that's what you should do.

Don't get out of order. I know some of you have strengths in certain areas and don't need as much help. Please don't skip ahead. This is a process that is meant to be followed in sequence. You may have thought that the order of the title was out of sequence. Some would think that the correct order should have been design, implement, and achieve. As you can see I teach it with the implementation last. That's because I feel that implementation is only truly accomplished if the achieved goal is sustainable. That's why implementation is last in the order. As you go through the sequence of this book, you will see that if you are proficient at one certain thing, you will finish it that much faster. I know that whenever I force myself to do things that I already think I am good at, I usually learn as much as ever. You just learn differently. Maybe you pick up on a nuance of something you have heard a million times and it just clicks. Sometimes the little things make all the difference. Well, to quote the trainer from Rocky, "What are we waiting for?" Good luck and Godspeed.

**Resource: You can download some actual mind maps and other great resources at our companion website. For more detailed information on these resources and real case study examples from this book, just go to page 179. You can get all the details there.

P.P.S.

Perfectly Precise Summary

1.) There are twelve Laws of Time that must be used in sequence.

2.) Some of these laws only manifest themselves in the mind.

3.) Other laws require action.

4.) These laws follow a pre-determined sequence but can be individually used at any time in the goal-achievement process.

5.) Mind Maps are a great way to map out your progress and see where you need help in any area.

Chapter 2

STOP! (Time) Thief
They do walk among us.

The alchemists had it right, kind of. All of their efforts for centuries focused on turning some other physical element into gold. There is an element that you can turn into gold at will. It's just not on the periodic table. It's not even in the normal three dimensions. That element is time, and once you master it, you can use that huge storehouse to manifest anything you want. Just like everything else in the physical universe, time is subject to laws and principles. One you obey those laws in the proper sequence, you can accomplish almost anything your heart desires. You can get rich if that is your desire. You can get more time off if you wish for that. You can become the great man or the great servant. Things that seemed only far-off in your imagination will become reality once you put good use to time. What good is wishing for something forever? Nothing good ever comes from wishing. Someone has to come forward, take charge, and lead people to achieve. When something great has been created, you can bet that the leader was enlightened to the ways of time and used the laws to their advantage. The laws of time will be there whether you use them or not. They were set into motion long ago, just like gravity or thermodynamics. What's the good news in all of this? Everyone on Earth has been given the same raw materials with which to work. As long as we are alive, we have the same chance to master these laws as anyone else. We all have the chance to make our dreams come true; we just have to pick a dream and apply these laws. It's as simple as that. Of course, there's a lot of work to do in following the proper sequence, but at least you will know you are on the right track. I can't wait to hear from the readers of this book at some point down the road, to find out what great mysteries have been solved and what great things have been done due to their understanding of these laws and their application. Good hunting!

To fully understand this book, I think a paradigm change of thought is needed. I will try to make the claim in these pages that the great accomplishments and fortunes of all history were bought and sold, not with dollar bills and gold coins but with minutes, seconds, and hours. You see, money is just a thing. It is probably better qualified as a thought about a thing. Years ago, paper money represented a nation's possession of precious metal in a vault somewhere. These days, money is less than worthless. It no longer has any intrinsic value besides the tradable value the government gives to it.

Throughout history, one thing has held true. Wealth does not come down from on high to lucky people. Just look at television shows about recent lottery winners. Most of these people were poor before they hit the lottery. Most were poor for good reason. After they won their millions, they slowly but surely headed back in the direction of poverty or mediocrity as quickly as they could. They couldn't hold on to their newfound gains because they hadn't earned their wealth with understanding. Across the span of time, the great ones have understood that there is really only one true currency in the world. Mastery of this currency will directly lead to the wealth that the master desires. This currency is available in limited supply to everyone. No one can purchase more of it with money, gold, jewels, or anything else. This currency has been divided equally among all humans with complete lack of prejudice. By now, you have figured out that the currency of which I am speaking is time.

Of course, some people stumble upon this truth before others. This gives them an advantage of sorts. Some people are afforded the luxury of not having to work for a living. This will free up some part of their day to spend their currency before it expires. These exceptions will always be there, but 99 percent of the people in the world never figure this stuff out. This means that just understanding where the true wealth lies in the universe will put you in the top 1 percent and set you on the road to greatness yourself.

The good news is that every day, you get your daily bank withdrawal of twenty-four hours. The bad news is that you only have those very same twenty-four hours to spend that time before it goes away forever. There is no way to invest that time. There is no miracle of compounding interest with this treasure. You have to spend it. Once you understand this, you are most of the way toward conquering your very dreams.

Today, we live in a world of distraction. The world appears to be speeding up, and there is nothing we can do about it. I propose that most of this is an illusion. Although things appear more hectic, that appearance is really a result of a shift in ideals and actions among us. We have decided to spend our daily allotment of time on different things than in the past. For example, many people love social media to the extent that they have chosen to make little useless communications between each other most of the day. Before the days of social media, they were spending their days doing something. One of the tragedies of our time is that we have built ever more elaborate networks and technologies, yet most people haven't a clue about the history behind any of the new developments they worship.

How many people could actually fix something if it broke? Yes, every third grader knows how to work their MP3 player, but who could fix it if it broke tomorrow? I know they are so cheap, we would just go buy another one, right? Well, that is the world in which we live right now, but for how long? If we don't start re-allocating some of our time to the study of principles and laws, we will find ourselves with little useful knowledge at some point in the future.

> *"Time is Money"* – **Benjamin Franklin**

We Say Time Is Money, But ...

If you understood the value of the time you were wasting, surely you wouldn't cast it aside like tossing a piece of paper in the garbage can. Who are some people who have gone on to great things after they came to understand? There are multitudes of people throughout history who are famous today because of what they did once they discovered the greatest hidden truth of all time. Thomas Edison was a clerk when he discovered the value of time and began studying electricity. He did that in his spare time. A man named Elihu Burritt was a blacksmith. He spent eleven hours a day in the backbreaking work of hammering away behind a scorching hot forge. Somehow he managed to master nineteen languages. Nineteen. William Shakespeare once managed a theater. Einstein once worked in a patent office. What did they all have in common? They did not waste their time. They viewed their spare time as the precious commodity it was and eventually became world famous for their accomplishments. It was once commonly said that successful people carried books around in their pockets so they could study and learn while they were doing things like riding the subway or waiting in a restaurant. I guess now most people have the capability to study on their Internet-ready cell phones. Most don't. They get distracted by all the bells and whistles. They see a post on their social networking account. Once there, they decide to make a flippant post on someone else's site. This comment is directed to a person, mind you, whom they wouldn't cross the street to warn of some impending danger. Still, they spend their precious daily allotment of time texting a few useless words.

We certainly don't need any help in wasting our precious wealth. However, if we can manage to get out or our own way, there are plenty of people there waiting to waste our time for us. If you were robbed on the street by a pickpocket, you would get upset and call the police. Let me ask you this question: how many of your friends will you gladly allow to outright rob you of your time? I am from the South, so I know a thing or two about being too polite. Here, we will routinely let someone approach us and steal our precious time. We won't say anything, because we don't want to be impolite. My own wife constantly accuses me of being rude because I don't spend extra time seeking out chitchat or social interaction. I battle this daily. I certainly don't want to be rude, but I have allocated specific amounts of time for each activity, and I just don't have the extra time to be extra social without stealing from myself in some other area. I do have a very short list of friends who I will allow to steal a moment or two from me. What do they all have in common? They all are high achievers who have a grasp on the value of time, both mine and their own. Therefore, when one of these guys calls up, I know it is for something worthwhile. Another lesson here is that you should pick your friends carefully if you plan to master time. This is harsh. You may have to redefine who you will let into your inner circle. When you feel bad about this, just remember the fact that your daily allotment of time is steadily ticking away. The people you begin to shy away from will not understand why. Maybe someday they will. Then you can gladly accept them back in with open arms.

> **Luke 15:23, 24:** *And bring hither the fatted calf, and kill it; and let us eat, and be merry: For this my son was dead, and is alive again; he was lost, and is found. And they began to be merry.*

Once they find the secret on their own, we can welcome them back. Until then, all efforts to convince them will probably be met with disbelief and hostility.

Time Stealers

This is not an exhaustive list of the types of people who will attempt to suck some of your precious time from you. I guess in this age of vampire popularity that is a good way to look at this. These types of people want to steal your time, in the hopes that they can use it for their own benefit. They can't actually use their time once they steal it, but it doesn't stop them from trying.

Non-thinkers

"If everyone is thinking alike, someone isn't thinking." —**Gen. George Patton**

This discipline of time stealers is one you may not run across if you are an extreme loner. However, once you enter into any type of relationship, you will quickly come across these people. I think in any relationship, someone will assume the role of leader and someone will assume the position of subordinate. This is natural and not all bad. There always has to be a leader. Everyone can't be the boss. True democracies rarely work for long. Having said that, I will add that the people who are in the relationship with the leader have to bring some value to the table. They cannot be complete non-thinkers.

Let's look at this relationship in the context of an employer and employee. Let's say that the boss has given a task to a certain employee to accomplish. The boss feels good about the delegation and goes on to the next item on the list for their day's achievements. The employee in question must be given good direction as to how to accomplish the task he has been assigned. That responsibility is squarely on the shoulders of the boss. Sometimes for some people, this is just not good enough. It wouldn't matter how great and precise the directions were for some people; they would still come to bother the boss. They simply don't have what it takes to make even the slightest little decision as the process moves forward. Sometimes it is even worse. Sometimes the employee with good instructions will still bother the boss to get "clarification." What does that mean? If the employee is following the instructions laid forth, there should be no need for clarification. Like I said, some people just don't trust themselves to make even the slightest variation of a decision on their own. I do believe you can coach these people to get better. To be mean, however, it would be a lot easier on you to just let them go. It doesn't mean they are a bad person or might not be great at a different job. It just means that you value your time so much that you don't want to spend any more of your limited amount on their training and encouragement.

Social Networkers

These people will make little innocuous statement on your accounts and hope for a response. It is doubtful that anything of value is ever said on one of these sites. Still, you may feel guilty if you don't respond to this trivial stuff. There is a place for social networking. In my opinion, the only good use is to improve your business workings. There is no way anyone needs to keep up with two hundred of their "closest" friends and all their meaningless musings. Another good question is, "Why would anyone want to keep up with me?" A subtype of social network time suckers is the person who continually updates his site with a blue million photos. They don't directly try to come for you, but they appeal to your weaknesses. They know that most of us can't resist looking into another's life to snoop around. They are more like enablers than anything else. If you're not careful, you will sit down at your computer to check a couple of things and come to your senses much later, having squandered several hours of your precious commodity. Another subtype of these particular stealers is the e-mail forwarder. Some people—who would otherwise be considered normal people—have fallen victim to this malady. I am not one, but I will attempt to assume why they do this. I suppose they are sitting there at their computer, checking e-mails, and they read one that has been forwarded to them. It may or may not have some cute little phrase that they want to share with everyone. Maybe it is something uplifting. Christian-themed e-mails are especially susceptible to forwarding. The e-mail forwarder may feel a little guilty for not forwarding it in this case. Sometimes the e-mail is more malicious. In this variety, the e-mail has some little sentence that claims something good (or bad) will happen or not, depending on whether or not the e-mail gets forwarded. Who gives the originator of this e-mail the right to threaten us with any particular outcome anyway? Once you get into the club of e-mail forwarding, I'm afraid you are there to stay unless you do something drastic. Most of the problems involving our participation with these time suckers involve our feelings of guilt if we don't comply. We don't want to hurt anyone else's feelings. Even deeper, we don't want to be rejected by these people, and we want to be liked. Just think about why you really participate, and decide if you want to trade them your precious time for theirs. I'll assure you they don't value their own time as much as you value yours.

Arguers

Some people are just contrarians. That is just their nature and there's not much you can do about it. I'm not talking about the people who have genuine concerns and want to explore all the options available before casting a final decision. Those people, however aggravating, are very useful in the decision-making process. I highly recommend that every leader keep one (notice, I said *one*) of these around to bounce new ideas off during the decision-making process. There is no place after the decision has been made for even one of these, and even your token naysayer should learn to keep his opinions to himself once the wheels have been set in motion on any project.

I am talking about the person who will be negative no matter what. This person loves to shoot holes in any new idea or theory that you might come up with. They thrive on controversy and love when they can insert strife into any conversation. It would be as rare as finding a tooth in the beak of a female chicken to find one of these people who has climbed to a high station in life or accomplished anything of lasting value. The secret truth is that most of these people wish they could achieve great things. They can't get past their own negativity or fear, so they love nothing more than to sabotage the workings of everyone they come in contact with. Where does all that negativity come from? It comes from a deep-seated fear. Maybe the person was hurt early in life by making a bold decision and has sworn to never try and fail again. Maybe a parent or other role model failed and convinced them from an early age to avoid risk. Whatever the precipitous event, the person is usually very fearful. They can't force themselves to take a chance, and they secretly despise the person who has the courage to move forward with a new idea or project. We will learn more about overcoming this in chapter 6.

There are lots of other time stealers lurking around you every day. We will address them when we come across specific examples while exploring the Twelve Laws. Just be aware that there is basically no end to the variations and imagination when it comes to stealing your time.

P.P.S.

Perfectly Precise Summary
  1.) Time wasting is an epidemic.
  2.) We must always be on guard for others wanting to steal our time.
  3.) There are several types of time "thieves" that we must learn to avoid.
  4.) No one ever accomplished anything truly great by wasting time.

Chapter 3

From Prussia with Love
The Most Efficient War Ever

L ess than two hundred years ago, a precise use of the Laws of Time changed the face of Europe and the world. As we tell the amazing story, I will point out just when each law was meticulously inserted into this war. Keep referring to this list until you have gotten the idea of how they used the laws.

Law 1 – Goals
Law 2 – Right Mind
Law 3 – Belief
Law 4 – Courage
Law 5 – Visual Learning
Law 6 – Operations
Law 7 – Logistics
Law 8 – Environment
Law 9 – Standard Operating Procedures
Law 10 – Discipline
Law 11 – Motivation
Law 12 – The Golden Rule

Just on the other side of the Elbe River lay a wasteland of sandy soil. A family of military adventurers had come to settle there and farm. They slowly built a province that would eventually topple all the nations in that part of Europe and shake the foundations of the entire Western world.

They did this by having complete mastery of all the Twelve Laws of Time. Let me tell the back-story and you'll soon see how the following of these laws gives unlimited power and chance for success in the face of unbelievable odds.

There are some characters who played their own part, and you should know who they are. The countries involved in this war were Prussia, the tiny state mentioned in the first paragraph, and France.

France was ruled by Louis Napoleon, nephew of the other Napoleon. Louis Napoleon had brought France back to being an empire again after the fall of his famous uncle. This Napoleon had led France to complete domination of European politics for about twenty years. At the time, France was the undisputed champion of Europe. No one dared challenge their military might. Their army was huge, well funded, well equipped, and experienced. Not to mention the fact that they had great weaponry for the day, with a crude early version of the machine gun. All this would give any country reason to doubt them as they tried to enact the Law of Belief.

Prussia was a tiny little kingdom about the size of the state of Colorado. It was run by King Wilhelm, one of the descendants of adventurers from long ago. Over the years, they had managed to place members of their family around Europe into different nations as rulers and kings. They were able to learn from the best that Europe had to offer and transfer some of that knowledge back to their ancestral home (Law 5: Visual Learning). Before the war began in the late 1800s, Prussia had become the main kingdom among several kingdoms and provinces that would eventually band together to become Germany after this war.

The mere fact that Prussia was in any position to even wage this war is amazing in and of itself. It didn't really have any of the resources the other nations of Europe had (another reason to doubt themselves). Prussia didn't have very many natural resources. The land there was sandy, barren, and lacking minerals. There weren't very many people. Towns were small and not close together. The country had no real culture or industry. Even the famous relatives of the king were relatively poor. These were all good reasons to doubt, yet they didn't (Law 3: Belief).

How, then, did this anomaly rise up and challenge the powers of the day for supreme authority? From way back, the common people and the nobility of Prussia had a common ideal (Law 1: Definite Ideal Goal). They wanted to grow their country by force. (This was a very specific way they wanted to grow it. Not a vague and fuzzy goal by any means.) By a demonstration of complete will power (Law 10: Discipline) and organizational genius (Law 7: Logistics), the royal family formed an army that would have made the Spartans of ancient times proud. (Law 2: Right Mind. They made sure that the army they built was really that good before they unleashed them.) That well-drilled army put one victory in front of another (Law 6: Operations), and before you knew it, an empire was born. Some people would say that Prussia was not a real nation with a real heritage because they depended on force of arms to build it. Their beauty was in the single-minded goals of their king (Law 1) and precision and attention to detail of their army (Law 6 and Law 9: Standard Operating Procedures). The king rewarded his army, reportedly spending five-sixths of all the countries income on it (Law 11: Motivation). It was said at the time that Prussia was not a country with an army, but an army with a country (Law 8: Environment). I'm sure that's the way the soldiers liked it. Maybe the other European nations were a little jealous. Still, everyone marveled at the factory-like efficiency of both the army and the state (Law 7). Citizens of Prussia were taught from an early age that they were expected to fit into the overall scheme of the king like a cog in a machine. Even the "philosophers" of Prussia preached obedience, duty, work, and sacrifice over self and self-interest. (Law 12: Golden Rule, kind of. Today, we wouldn't think so, but at this time in history, the actions of nation above self were much more likely to enact this rule than today.)

The Prussian leaders were not men of leisure. Most of them ran large estates with farming and livestock and worked tirelessly in those efforts. Like we said earlier, there were no cities or towns of any real size to allow true civilization to crop up. This fostered the growth of independent, talented thinkers (very capable of following Law 2: Right Mind). One other thing Prussians were known for besides war was business. Many of them were able to turn quite a profit from those farms and estates out in the country, which would have been quite the feat in those days.

Out of this environment came two men whose successes led them to become primary advisors to the king and the heroes of the most efficient war in history. These men weren't afraid to act on their true belief that Prussia could become a world power (Law 4: Courage).

The first one was Prince Otto von Bismarck, Chancellor of Prussia. The other, Count Helmuth von Moltke, was a general in the army and architect of the war plan.

To pull off this stunning upset, they needed several things. First, they had to have a definite plan (Law 1). They needed a standard or Definite Ideal Goal to go by.

Second, they needed an organization capable of attaining and maintaining the ideals through the application of principles (Laws 6, 7, and 9).

Third, they needed equipment, men, money, materials, machines, and methods to enable the organization, through the application of principles, to attain and maintain the ideals.

Fourth, they needed leaders, competent and forceful, making the organization and equipment attain and maintain ideals.

Whether consciously or not, this was a perfect imitation of the Laws of Time at work. You can also see these laws displayed in each one of us if you just think about it. Human life is amazingly efficient. The body is the organization. All the sense organs, limbs, and appendages are the equipment, and the brain is the leader of it all. Many times, nature will show you the most efficient and effective way if you just have the ability to look and see.

Those two leaders, Bismarck and Moltke, had the ideal setup that consisted of a powerful and unified Prussian state, with their king at its head. Each of these leaders created his own respective organizations, military and diplomatic. They equipped their organizations and made them powerful enough to realize those ideals (Law 8: Environment). They couldn't count on having as many men, as much money, as abundant equipment, or as much material as their opponents. However, it was evident to them that belief in their invisible theories and principles, which their self-sufficient enemies did not realize until too late, would have to make up for their deficit in material resources, manpower, and equipment.

This war was, from its very beginning and planning, going to be one of efficiency versus inefficiency. Prussia adeptly applied all twelve laws to their plan through their new conception and shaping of their military organization.

To show how thoroughly Prussia had planned this war with France, let's go back a few years before that war and see how Prussia tried out their theories on one of their own. This squarely falls under the Law of Operations.

For a long time, there had been a disputed territory between Prussia and Denmark. There were actually two provinces there in question.

Bismarck picked a fight with Denmark and invited Prussia's next-door sister country, Austria, to join in. This gave Moltke a couple of chances to put into action all the plans he had been practicing with the Prussian army. First, he tried it out on poor little Denmark. They offered very little resistance, but that was to be expected. Then there was a little trickery by Bismarck. He suggested that Prussia should occupy one of the newly conquered territories and Austria should occupy the other. Sounds generous, right?

Prussia was definitely smaller than Austria, with 22 million people, as opposed to Austria's 59 million. That didn't stop Bismarck. He then picked a fight with Austria over the newly acquired territory that he had suggested Austria occupy in the first place. Moltke had been carefully studying the tactics of the Confederacy from the American Civil War. He definitely thought he knew how not to fight a larger power. Two years to the day after the Battle of Gettysburg, and with remarkable precision, Prussia marched 225,000 men against Austria's 262,000 men. Three weeks later, Austria begged for a truce. If you looked at that war as a business venture, Austria had to pay Prussia nearly 800 billion in today's dollars and gave them 27,000 square miles of real estate for the three-month investment. It is unlikely that any corporation in the world will ever equal that venture, strictly in terms of return on investment.

What Napoleon and France failed to realize in all of this was that the two wars Prussia had just waged were nothing more than non-conference or preseason games in preparation for the big showdown with them. All Bismarck, Moltke, and Prussia were waiting for was a sliver of daylight and an opportunity to strike against their old rival, France.

Well, it came in the form of something so modest that you can scarcely believe France fell for it. The Prussian royal family had been placing members of their family on thrones and in positions of authority all over Europe. More than likely, it was just the way things were done in those days and not some detailed plan at that point in time. Of course, it could have been an evil master plan; who knows? King Wilhelm had a nephew, Prince Leopold, whom Spain had asked to be their king. He said he would. There only delay was that the Spanish legislative body had to approve his rule. When Napoleon found out about this, he was mortified. Spain was to his west and Prussia was to his east. Would this mean that he would now have rivals on both sides that were in cahoots with each other? Now Napoleon got upset and started making demands of Prussia.

Little did Napoleon know that Bismarck and Moltke had been carefully drawing up their plans for a long time. Prussia had only 300,000 regular troops at their disposal, and France had nearly 500,000.[3] I'm sure that Napoleon thought that Prussia wouldn't really dare attack him. He also probably believed that if Prussia were so foolish, they would be crushed within days. Prussia had been busy, though. Bismarck had been making strategic alliances, and though not as well-drilled as Prussian troops, he had the availability to call upon troops from some of the lesser German countries to help, and they had plans for that. Prussia had made it a top priority to improve their railroads and was far ahead of France in their ability to deploy.

On July 19, 1870, France finally declared war on Prussia. It has been said that when the word arrived to Moltke, he was asleep. When awakened, he simply said, "You will find the plan of campaign in the third drawer of my desk." He then rolled over and went back to sleep. Can you imagine? What level of confidence Moltke had in his plan and the ability of his men to carry it out. From that point in time, every man in Prussia and their allied states stepped, ate, and filled every moment of their time according to a pre-arranged schedule. This is the invocation of the Law of Standard Operating Procedure to the highest. They were called from their homes and private businesses everywhere throughout

---

3   http://en.wikipedia.org/wiki/Franco-Prussian_War

the kingdom. All railroads fell in line with all their equipment. There was no confusion, no hysterics, and no silly haste. The citizens found their uniforms and weapons ready and their provisions stored. French plans called for mobilization of their army in nineteen days. Moltke's plan called for mobilization in eighteen days. He knew that if he could get there first, the war could be fought primarily in France. The way it actually turned out was that France could only get going in twenty-one days, while Prussia was true to plan and was war-ready in eighteen days,[4] 100 percent efficient. Exactly one month after the first battle was fought, Napoleon himself was captured, his army beaten, and the war was over, for all intents and purposes.

Moltke knew all twelve of the Laws of Time. For him, war was a serious business undertaking, and because it was a business venture, Prussia presented France with the bill and collected payment. France paid Prussia 25 trillion in today's dollars and gave them two French provinces to boot. Once again, an amazing profit if you consider this strictly a business venture like the Prussians did.

To observers of that war, it was not the pomp and glory that was intriguing. There was little of either. It was the calm, merciless skill of the Prussian plan that most impressed. It showed what the Laws of Time could do when carried out to the nth degree by a competent organization. It was not the Prussian army who won the war. Bismarck and Moltke would have won equally as impressively if they had applied those principles to the armies of Italy, Russia, America, or even France. The Prussian soldiers were not the most enthusiastic side in the war. In fact, their esprit de corps was well below that of French soldiers. Once, while witnessing a failed French cavalry charge from atop a hill, King Wilhelm was overheard to say, "Those brave men." Don't underestimate them; they were enthusiastic enough. Try fighting for

---

4   Werstein, Irving. *The Franco-Prussian War; Germany's rise as a world power.*
Julian Messner, Division of Pocket Books, Inc. New York, NY, 1965.

your life if you aren't extremely motivated. It's just that the French soldiers also possessed this quality in spades.

In the end, it was not the Prussian drills or maneuvers that won the day. It was not the Prussian equipment; remember, it was slightly less advanced than French weaponry. It was not Prussian money that won the war. France was far richer and had far more credit. France had a lot going for it. If only they had applied *all* the laws to the degree of their opponents, the outcome would surely have been different. There was one law that Prussia used to a decided advantage throughout all stages of the conflict. It was their organization and their logistics that won the day.

Prussia had supplemented the old type of military organization and had understood and applied all twelve of the Laws of Time to their benefit. In this way, they will forever be remembered for carrying out one of the all-time greatest ventures in the history of the world—military, business, or otherwise. They also chalked up a win for underdogs everywhere when they did it.

P.P.S.

Perfectly Precise Summary
1.) The Laws of Time will work in a small endeavor or a large complex undertaking like a war.
2.) Even the biggest underdog can use these laws to succeed against all odds.
3.) All twelve laws must be followed for complete success.

Chapter 1

===

Law 1: Goals
Goals Are Worthless ...

I am cringing as I type this, because it was a monumental leap for me personally to go from a time in my life when I had no goals to a time when I had clearly written and defined goals. Just the fact that I wrote them down meant so much to me. Once I had a clear vision of what things I wanted in life, I was then free to go out and get them. For the most part, I have achieved all the goals that I set out for myself several years ago when I discovered this for the first time.

The rich reward of time cannot be realized without clear goals. Without the framework of goals, time will wander wastefully around and never reach any destination. Have you ever said or thought, "I wonder where all the time went?" That was time without clear direction. Time didn't have a goal to point toward with a deadline in which to accomplish it. We must give time the direction it needs to allow it to work in our favor. It is necessary that we give time a fighting chance and obey the first law.

Even though we know that adherence to the Twelve Laws of Time will guarantee success, we also acknowledge that most people will not have the inner strength to complete their mission and see their goal become reality. Consider Moses. This was a man who people of all faiths would consider a great leader. He was equipped with *the* ten laws that would give any followers complete success in this life. Moses came down from his meeting with his boss to his people's temporary offices. The headman, God, had even taken the time to write his Standard Operating Procedure down on stone tablets so there could be no confusion or misinterpretation. Moses took his time reading them slowly and placing emphasis on just the right spots. Surely his organization would see the light, listen, practice the laws, and become perfect. God had told Moses that they couldn't move into their new, amazing offices on the Mediterranean until the laws were followed completely. Surely this would be motivation enough. The new offices even had a name that marketers would find hard to trump, the Promised Land. Well, Moses ran into some setbacks. There was a strong faction of sub-grouping that had gained a foothold while he was in his meeting. They had even tried to gain support for a new CEO by building a statue in his honor. Moses couldn't believe it. He had in his hands the tool that his people needed to be successful, and they just weren't going to have it. I'm sure that everyone thought the ten laws of Moses were good ideas; they just weren't instinctive to these people. They didn't feel right to them. I'm sure they felt like they were just too tough to follow through on. That's why Moses, stuck with this bunch for forty years of wandering, griping, and moaning, finally got so aggravated that he broke one of the head man's lesser rules himself. I have always thought that if I were Moses, I would have broken more than one minor rule. Still, Moses didn't get fired, but he didn't get to move into his fancy corner office in Canaan, either. He was kept out in the field, while a young gun, Joshua, was chosen to head up the new home office.

If this was the outcome for Moses, one of the greatest leaders of all times, with the help of God himself, what can we expect to accomplish? Luckily, the Laws of Time are very simple and easy to follow. They take time and effort, but what good ever came from anything that didn't? If followed correctly, they will lead you to achieve any goal you desire. Now, I want you to promise me right now that you won't use these twelve laws for evil. These will lead you to success, whatever your motives, but I can't bear the thought of helping someone accomplish some nefarious goal. If you do that, I will hunt you down and personally read you the Bible, and then make you apologize to everyone you hurt in the process. If you need any help determining whether or not your intentions are good, you might look up the aforementioned laws of Moses in the aforementioned Bible for guidance. Now, where was I? Ah, yes, goals.

One of my ten-year goals from 2002 was to become a public speaker. Not only that, but to speak on my own terms. That was important to me then, and it is important to me now. I always knew that I didn't want to be one of those guys who flew to a different city twice each week. I'm sure you can build a business like no other in that way. It is an old-school tried-and-true method to get your name out there and get people who like you to want to give you money. There's no question I believed that, but I wanted some sanity in my life. I only wanted to speak a few times a year. I also only wanted to speak to a select few groups, not everyone everywhere.

I believe I have accomplished this goal. As of this writing, I am only accepting about one speaking engagement every three months or so. I have had only the best very select audiences of dentists who share (for the most part) my way of thinking. I have had great success selling to these people because I have offered them something that appeals to their sensibilities and their inner beliefs. Next year I will be able to give two lectures in Orlando in three days and give my family a weeklong vacation at the theme parks to boot.

Only seven short years ago, I had no prospects of speaking. No company of which to speak. No idea how to get there. I only had the dream and goal of doing this someday. It was a dream that would have certainly seemed improbable to anyone in attendance at the Chalybeate Elementary eighth-grade graduation, where I suffered stage fright so bad while attempting to give the valedictory address that my lungs locked up. I could only take in one breath during the entire speech. I somehow squeaked out Robert Frost's "The Best Is Yet to Be," before stumbling, light-headed, back to my folding chair. It would have seemed equally hard to believe if you heard me four years later at my high school graduation. Another valedictory address was given. Another disaster occurred. This time I forgot my lines and my brain was in such a state of disrepair that I literally couldn't read the index cards that could have saved the day. I stammered enough incoherent sentences to get through it somehow. Luckily for me, no one really listens to these speeches anyway.

In college, I was too scared to even attempt taking speech class during the regular session and took it in the summer sessions with the jocks and other folks too scared to face the real teachers. I managed my way through the class, but to no fanfare. I would have been one of the last folks anyone would have expected to speak from the stage, but here I am still. Now I speak to rooms filled with hundreds of my peers. I'm not the best, but I'm not the worst either. Why am I here? I think it is that little goals sheet I made out those seven years ago.

So I'm not bashing goals altogether. They can get you pretty far in life. Maybe they can get you as far as you want to go. Let's look at what makes up these superficial goals, and then I'll let you in on what I think really makes you tick. The understanding of the latter can open up some amazing doorways in your life. But first, let's give the old-fashioned understanding of goals its due.

There is no way that any course on time management or the use thereof could even take a little baby step forward without considering some basic principles.

This first law is governed by the ability to make your goals clear in your mind. I don't mean just clear, like see-through-a-windowpane clear. I mean crystal clear. I mean ultimate high-definition clear. This also only works if you define your own crystal-clear goals.

There are many types of goals out there. Let's go over a few.

The Low Goal — This goal may or may not be clear. It is usually something set with a bar intentionally low. Sometimes these kinds of goals are set just for the sake of setting a goal because someone has heard that goals are good things to have. People who set easily achievable goals really have no true respect for the power of the Law of Goals, because there is, in their mind, a good chance that they would have reached this goal even if they had never clearly defined it. This is setting a goal just for the sake of setting one. I certainly think it is a waste of a good universal law.

The Sideways Goal — This type of goal is set in such a way that the end result is not very much of an improvement on the current situation. It may very well even be that the end result is already there. Maybe it is not apparent to all parties, but it is already there. This is kind of like a person who owns his own company saying that his goal is to create a new position in the office. Chances are that this office already exists de facto and just doesn't have the name. It would then be easy to meet this goal by simply naming the position. This might well have been a good goal in another's hands. Maybe someone who needed to learn to delegate to take a little weight off their shoulders would have profited more. This would have involved interviewing and hiring a good person. Then you would have developed a system and job description for the job and trained the right person. Then you would have slowly been able to trust them with more and more complicated intricacies of your core business. This would have yielded you the ability to step away from the office more and feel secure about doing so. This is the key to a *real* clearly defined goal, and I'll talk about that later in this chapter. Hopefully you can see the difference in the value of the two goals I described, even though they might look exactly the same in writing.

The Vague Goal — This is a very dangerous thing. You mind will begin to subconsciously work toward the attainment of any goal you put in place. That's why it is vitally important to be crystal clear. The vague goal gives the mind a general idea of what you want. It just doesn't give specifics or good reasons for the goal. An example of this would be wanting to get in better shape. I know—who doesn't? How is your mind supposed to interpret this? It probably will bog itself down with the multitude of possibilities, and you will not lose an ounce of weight or gain an ounce of muscle. A better goal would have been that you wanted to lose twenty pounds in ninety days. During the same period of time, you would like to have successfully completed twenty pull-ups and one hundred push-ups in a row without stopping. You would have also have liked to have completed a 5K run during those ninety days.

Now that is not a vague goal. This is something your mind can really grab a hold of.

The Unrealistic Goal — I intentionally downplay the discussion of this type of goal because I am one of those starry-eyed dreamers who believe that anything is possible in life with the right amount of effort. Having said that, there are some times when you should really think hard about your goals before you write them down. For example, if you were born outside the United States, maybe you shouldn't make becoming the president a serious goal for yourself. I don't doubt that you could become a very high-level official in politics, but to become president, the Congress would have to change the laws of the land. I'm not saying this would be impossible, but let's just keep it a little realistic. I'm all for the big, outrageous goal, just keep it real. I have a pet saying: "Set yourself up for success." I believe that you should always be on the lookout for ways to make your successes effortless. This would not mean that you should never aim high; just stay on the planet. Don't ask the laws of physics to cease to exist for your goal to come true. One of my favorite Bible verses is Matthew 17:20, where Jesus says, "For verily I say unto you, If ye have faith as a grain of mustard seed, ye shall say unto this mountain, Remove hence to yonder place; and it shall remove; and nothing shall be impossible unto you." Now, if Jesus says something, I believe it. That doesn't mean that I'm going to go over to the Grand Tetons and start pushing on a rock at the base of the mountains. If God himself bellows that order out from a cloud, I'll go start pushing. Until then, I'll keep that action off my list of clearly defined goals.

The Impromptu Goal — This type of goal is one that is not well thought out. It can be impulsive. It is usually emotional. Now, I don't say that emotion is a bad thing when you are forming your goals. You must simply channel the energy of the enthusiasm into constructive areas and let your logical mind walk you through the potential consequences of setting a particular goal. It is very possible to set an impromptu goal quickly and set on down the path of achieving that goal without giving the proper thought to what you will do once you get there. Also, you might get halfway and decide that you really don't like the direction and the end result has become less appealing than when you began your journey. It is for this reason that I wholeheartedly recommend thoughtful consideration before finalizing any goal. Once you set that goal down and commit to it, your mind will attempt to reach it, whether or not the desired outcome is in the best interest of yourself or others.

The Definite Ideal Goal — This is the best of the types of superficial goals out there. Great things have been accomplished by those who managed to form this definite ideal. Even if the last little ingredient that we will speak on in a moment wasn't involved, the power of this goal will almost always bring forth at least the desired outcome. There are two acid tests for determining if you have come up with a Definite Ideal Goal (DIG). The first is that the desired outcome can be understood and grasped by yourself and others. This means that someone could look at the end product of your goal and say to themselves, "You know what, that is a real accomplishment." The second is that you or other people can look at the end result and say with all honesty and sincerity that the end result of the goal is a consequential thing, something of value. The end result must accomplish some real purpose other than mere existence. There is no real value to a goal that, when accomplished, serves no real purpose in the world.

There is no way now to determine if the achievers who drew up the plans for the Seven Wonders of the Ancient World used the secret extra seasoning from the end of the chapter when they originally drew up their plans and set forth their goals. I do think anyone with any sense will look at their example and say that they did fulfill the acid tests required to enter membership into the DIG Society. Let's look at a couple.

The oldest set of wonders built by humankind is the pyramids of Egypt. The last wonder of the ancient world was the great lighthouse at Alexandria. Not only were these massive structures built to last, but they had a purpose and a value. The purpose of the pyramids was to give the ancient kings and queens of Egypt a place to lie in state forever, or at least until their resurrection. They also gave the country pride and became a sign to all the world of the might that Egypt possessed at that time. The lighthouse of Alexandria had the purpose of directing the bulk of the floating commerce of the ancient world. Its value came from the accomplishment of its task to keep that city at the heart of the world at that time as a business powerhouse. I also submit to you that these and the other wonders of that time held some value greater than just their accomplished task. Whether pride, love, beauty, or hope, a Definite Ideal Goal will give exponentially more than just the desired result.

Now, what about the little secret I promised you throughout this chapter?

I believe that to give ourselves amazing amounts of energy toward the achievement of any goal, we have to dig a little deeper than those superficial things we all imagine from the outset. Anyone can imagine a goal of driving a fancy sports car. Anyone can imagine earning a million dollars. Those things are fine, but *why* do you want to obtain those goals? Have you sat down and really thought this through? What would you do with the million dollars if you got it, anyway?

You have to come up with the reasons all on your own, but you must decide why you want any object of desire. In reality, things are just things. Things don't buy you happiness. Emotions buy you happiness. Maybe you want the million dollars because you want more security for your family. Maybe you want the million dollars because you want to feel accepted by your peers. Acceptance and security are far more powerful motivators for your subconscious than just money and houses. That's the key. You have to move past the visualization of the object to the inner workings of why the thing is so important to you. Now, I said before that the Law of Goals would work without this added bonus secret. That's true, it will, but why would you not delve just a little deeper when you are so close to the real prize?

An added bonus for those of us who own businesses is this. If you, as the boss, form a DIG and stick to it, your goal will permeate the entire company and greatly increase efficiency. One of the great production killers in existence today is the lack of employees' understanding of the Definite Ideal Goal of the company or the boss. Once that is completely crystallized for the employee, they can move forward with an internal compass and accomplish more than could have been possible when only vague guesses of the company's desires existed.

When you figure out just exactly what you really want and why, your power becomes so much greater. Now you are setting yourself up for success, and effortless success at that. Your mind will become freer than you could possibly imagine when you become clear on this one thing, and that will make the goal achievement come that much faster. I think the Greeks got it right centuries ago with an inscription over their great temple of Apollo at Delphi. They simply chiseled, "Know thyself."

Going back to the title of the chapter, I think it is obvious that goals are not worthless. That was just my way of exaggerating to make this point. Goals can get you specific results. This has been proven again and again throughout history. By digging deeper into your psyche, you can unlock a powerful secret that will make the attainment of those goals much easier and the results much more powerful than would be possible without this extra exercise.

Now go to the workshop portion for Law 1 and get started.

P.P.S.

Perfectly Precise Summary
1.) Goals must be precisely defined.
2.) The Definite Ideal Goal is precise enough to be achieved.
3.) You must understand the unclear goal types so you can test yours to make sure it is attainable.

Chapter 2

Law 2: Right Mind
Use your head for something besides a hat rack.

The Law of the Right Mind is something that must be obeyed before you can move forward into the next phases of Time Genius. When you obey the Right Mind, you will have a crystal-like clarity that your objective is worthy and true. You will have filtered out all the impurities from the goal you have set for yourself. You will have to be brutally honest with yourself, and you must dump out any inaccurate, wrong, superstitious, or crazy ideals that have accumulated in yourself.

You will leave this chapter with the knowledge that you are on the right path and that your goal is one that is worthy of achievement and success. Once you master the Right Mind, you will no longer be susceptible to bad advice, because you will have learned how to listen to the truth and make proper decisions and adjustments based on that truth.

Simply knowing that you have made a good decision and are thinking with a right mind will set up the bridge to an unshakable core belief and will lead you into the next chapter.

> *"Nothing astonishes men so much as common sense and plain dealing."*
> **– Ralph Waldo Emerson**

Common Sense

An interesting thing, this common sense. Everyone certainly believes that they possess all the common sense they might need while traveling this earth. Most believe that they possess this trait in superior quantity to most of their peers. Just look at any audience when a comedian tells a joke about someone not having much common sense. Everyone laughs. Why do they laugh? One would assume that everyone laughing at the joke thinks that they have common sense aplenty and know lots of people who they think don't have very much. I don't say that this self-appreciation is a bad thing. People need self-confidence. People need to believe in themselves, as we talk about in the next chapter. Without this belief in one's own common sense, not much would get done. Having said that, there are many failures around us that could have been averted with a little bit of the common sense that everyone thinks they own in spades. Why is that?

I believe that most people are actually born with a good bit of common sense. Maybe that's how it got its name. The problem comes when people let a whole lot of "stuff" cloud the flow of the common sense into whatever goal or project in which they are involved. The stuff to which I refer is mostly learned. Traditions, conditions, current practice models, and immediate "needs" can detour even the best-laid plan if a person doesn't apply common sense to the equation.

Let's look at a couple of examples from the business world. From my industry, let's look at the case of a doctor—let's call him Fred—who is in his fifties. This doctor has nearly paid off his dental office loans, has some retirement socked away, and may have his house paid off. The doctor makes a few hundred thousand dollars a year but invests lots of that back into his business. Sometimes the purchases pay off and sometimes they don't. Fred still has enough money lying around to enjoy a good lifestyle and will really be able to save toward retirement when the dental office is finally paid off.

Then, Fred reads about a hotshot dentist in another state, about Fred's age or younger, who has this Taj Mahal-like office building on an expensive real estate lot. This thing is so huge that it resembles a bank. Photos of the inside reveal that the Taj Mahal may not have been a good comparison. The dental office is much nicer. The floors are marble. The counters are granite, not that imitation stuff you can get at the home supply store. The dental equipment is immaculate. It looks as if you could eat off the floor of each dental procedure operatory. All the staff are wearing matching black outfits, and most of them look like they have weekend jobs as models for fashion catalogs. The doctor in the pictures is smiling like the Cheshire cat. From the looks of the shot of the parking lot, he drives a heck of a sports car as well. Boy, life looks good in those photos. Fred starts to wonder what life would be like on the other side of that fence. What would it be like to have that office? What would it be like to coach that staff? I'll bet the dentistry would even be better and easier on those patients, wouldn't it? Fred begins to fall in love with this portrayed ideal in the magazine spread. He begins to believe that if he just built that type of practice, all his dreams would come true.

Fred thinks about it, but his common sense is clouded by issues like pride, envy, and just plain old misinformation. Lack of information is also a problem. Did the doctor in the magazine have a mortgage? The article didn't say. Did the practice cash flow well? The article didn't say that either. Fred goes against his common sense and decides that he wants to build this type of practice so badly that he doesn't care what the true answers to this are. Then Fred decides that he will use the concept of social proof to back up his new idea, instead of common sense. Fred decides that since several doctors have appeared in several issues of different trade magazines, they must all be doing well. Of course, this train of thought is all wrong, but Fred is hell-bent to go through with this thing, and no filter of common sense is being used. Fred goes to the bank and asks for a loan of more than 1 million dollars for his new dream office. It will have the best of everything. The banker could stop all of this, but since Fred's credit is good and his income is pretty high, he gladly gives him the loan. You see, the banker doesn't care that Fred will have to work until he dies to pay this loan off. He knows that Fred has the ability to make the monthly payments as long as he can totter to work. Heck, Fred can probably afford this note even if his assistant has to wheel him from room to room on a doctor's stool. The loan is made.

Now Fred is free to enjoy his dream. The only problem is that once the building is built, Fred is stuck. No one in their right mind will come in to buy this big old place to take it off his hands, because it is so nice. In fact, it is so nice that the only people who could really afford to pay what it is worth would probably rather pay extra and get their building personalized to fit their own whims and style. Fred now has a monthly note that is outrageous compared to the one he was nursing toward finality before all of this. Fred's overhead is much higher. Now it takes a much bigger percentage of the practice's profits to get all the bills paid. Even though the office is well liked by the patients, the office doesn't make that much more money. This puts a stress on Fred, and he passes this stress off onto his staff. They may be pretty, but they're ticked off and on edge most of the time. Fred can no longer save for retirement the way he wants to. He hides this from his wife and doesn't let on to his kids, but the stress eats at him and he becomes unhealthier than he has ever been. All this at exactly the wrong time in his life. Fred's take-home pay has shrunk to nearly nothing. He has trouble keeping up with the lifestyle he used to have, even before this latest venture. Fred drops a couple of non-essential luxuries from his life, like the country club membership or the waterskiing boat. Fred tells anyone who asks that he just didn't have time to play golf or go to the lake anymore, but that life has never been better.

The dental supply representative who sold Fred all this beautiful, top-notch equipment senses that things aren't as great as Fred is letting on and feels a little bad about profiting so much on Fred's bad decision. He calls the home office and tells them that one of his best customers has just built this amazing, state-of-the-art dental office and that it features so much of their company's equipment that it would be good for one of their monthly practice-of-the-month feature articles in their trade magazine. After seeing the exquisite photos of Fred's office, the dental supply company agrees. They set up the photo shoot with Fred and his staff. All of Fred's crew are miserable, but they do like the idea of all those other dental practices seeing the pictures and being jealous of them, so they put on their best face. Fred feels a little bit like a hypocrite. He knows that his situation isn't as good as he has been letting on, but he is still proud. He also feels like he has earned his moment in the sun for all the money, time, and trouble he has spent to own this fur-lined coffin. For one shining moment, Fred and his staff pull themselves together, look straight at the camera, and smile like they are at a party at the Ritz. If you look closely at Fred, he is smiling just like the Cheshire cat.

Now, what could Fred have done differently to avoid all this anguish? Certainly, there are people in the world who own nice dental offices and do quite well financially. Fred's big problem was not using common sense or the Law of Right Mind to think things through properly. Fred let emotion dictate his final actions. Emotions are very useful in another chapter we will cover, but not this one. You must make your final decision based on cold, hard facts and instincts. Fred could have stayed in his old dental office for a couple of years and paid off all his notes. Then he could have socked away thousands each month into his savings accounts, to the point where he could retire at any time. Then he could have chosen to walk away, or if it really was a dream of his to have a nice dental office, he could have started a savings account to pay for the nicer practice, albeit not a Taj Mahal. His life would have surely been happier and less stressful.

Lots of businesses make the same mistakes as Fred. Many approach their business like the famous kid who wanted to start a lemonade stand. This one kid in particular really wanted to make some extra money for the summer. He had quite a lot saved already, but he wanted some more. The only flaw in his plan was that he thought he needed the best of everything before he ever opened up to his first customer.

This kid used his savings to buy the nicest lemon squeezers, ice pulverizers, strainers, shakers, tables, and tents. He had the nicest cups he could buy. He used only organic sugar from sugar canes grown on chemical-free farms in California. The pitchers were only the purest crystal he could find. He hired a marketing expert to design his sign to go in front of his fancy table. The water he bought to use was purified from melting glaciers at the North Pole.

There was only one problem. By the time the kid had bought everything else, he had spent all his savings. He didn't have one more dime to buy even one lemon. He never saw his first customer. If he had seen a customer, he would have had to charge so much that his buddy down the street with the old poker table and fresh-squeezed lemonade in sticky glasses would have gotten all the business because he could charge a quarter and make a profit.

These are good examples of lack of judgment in business, but what about time? The thread of common sense runs through any decision you make. It runs through every project you begin and every efficient strategy you come up with. You must exercise common sense to be successful in all your endeavors.

If you are planning on improving your quality of life by mastering some portion of your day with better time management, you had darn sure better be cognizant of this law. You simply cannot improve your time in any area if you are blindly holding on to some tradition that may no longer hold any value. You cannot get faster or quicker if you are performing unnecessary steps in the process just because someone told you to or you think they have to be done. Think every step through before you form your final plan and you will be the wiser for it in the end.

Yes, better methods and processes are the ultimate goal of any idea. However, individually they are only a small cog in the wheel. To fully grasp the concept of *Time Genius*, you must shake off the shackles of tradition and pull free from the quicksand of the "crowd" and adopt a new line of thought. This new way of thinking will ultimately free you in ways you can't believe if you apply the law of the Right Mind.

Rate-limiting Factors

Ever since I was a pre-dental student in college, I have come across things that I have identified as rate-limiting steps or rate-limiting factors. Lord knows I had to deal with them a lot in the eight different chemistry classes I took. I think people have rate-limiting factors, too. Just think about it; you probably think you just cannot do something or other because of a deep-down belief that you hold. You may not even know that you hold that belief, but it's holding you back. More than likely, you are housing a whole bunch of these rate-limiting beliefs in your psyche. The problem is that you base all future decisions off the more deeply held limiting beliefs. Soon, you may have an entire train of decisions and beliefs that have a faulty foundation deeply embedded down there somewhere. It could even be just one little brick of the foundation that is bad, but the whole building has been constructed to fit over that weak spot. If you have one of those rate-limiting factors or beliefs down there, you probably have a weaker house than you could enjoy if you had the proper right mind about that particular belief.

You must make sure when you are forming your plan of action that you aren't hindering your progress with one of these limiting beliefs. Let's look at an example from the past that makes a lot of sense in this area. Everyone has heard the story of Roger Bannister breaking the four-minute-mile barrier. If you break down that glorious victory, you see that he was simply trying to master a time problem. He had a process, the mile run, which he wanted to achieve more efficiently. He had to go through all the stages that we have identified as laws of time to achieve his ultimate goal. At some point, he had to put behind him the rate-limiting belief that the four-minute barrier was impossible for human beings. He had plenty of intelligent people backing him up with the agreed truth that it was impossible to run it in that amount of time. All the other runners at the time believed it was impossible too. At some point, Bannister removed that weak brick from his foundational beliefs and ran that mile in less than four minutes. Guess what? After he removed the rate-limiting belief, lots of others ran it in less than four minutes. He had forced them to rethink their beliefs and rebuild their strategies to improve on their times. This is one definite application of the Right Mind Law.

P.P.S.

Perfectly Precise Summary

1.) You must be honest with yourself about the goal you desire.

2.) If it is something unbelievably impossible (although most are not), rethink your Pre-Goal and start over.

3.) Understand and define your Rate-limiting Factors and guard against them.

Chapter 3

Law 3: Belief
Go Tell it on the Mountain

> **Matthew 17:20:** *And Jesus said unto them, Because of your unbelief: for verily I say unto you, If ye have faith as a grain of mustard seed, ye shall say unto this mountain, Remove hence to yonder place; and it shall remove; and nothing shall be impossible unto you.*

Countless pages, volumes, books, and reports have been recorded throughout human history cheering the power of belief. I certainly believe in belief. That sounds weird, but it is true. I hope to convince you that you must believe in whatever you are trying to achieve if you hope to be successful.

Let's look at a wonderful outlaying of that philosophy by Ralph Waldo Trine:

"Faith, absolute dogmatic faith, is the only law of true success. When we recognize the fact that a man carries his success or his failure with him, and that it does not depend upon outside conditions, we will come into the possession of powers that will quickly change outside conditions into agencies that make for success. When we come into this higher relation and bring our lives into complete harmony with the higher laws, we will then be able so to focus and direct the awakened interior forces that will go out and return

laden with that for which they are sent. We will then be great enough to attract success, and it will not always be apparently just a little ways ahead."

Those words were written almost a century ago, yet they still ring true. Belief is a law of thought, but it is still a law. It would be a rare case indeed if someone accomplished something of significance and did not believe in himself.

The reason that belief is so important in the sequence of accomplishment is that no one realizes the difficulties they will encounter at the beginning of a journey. Everything's a journey, isn't it? Even the most mundane improvements in the efficiency of one little procedure are ultimately a journey. So, let's look at the beginning of the journey. Let's say that to accomplish a feat, you must climb over a mountain and get to the valley on the other side. The other side will represent an objective that you want to meet or a goal you want to achieve. The journey starts out pleasantly enough. You may be walking in sunlight, in comfortable weather, enjoying the scenery of the mountain upcoming. From here, the mountain doesn't look all that tough. It may even look beautiful. You are probably thinking that this is going to be an easy journey. Think again. Soon enough, you start to walk uphill. That makes things a little harder, but not all that difficult. Then, as you continue on your way, you climb to higher elevations and the weather turns cooler. Maybe the sun hides behind the clouds. This makes things even a little tougher. You manage to fight onward, but things are definitely not as easy as they seemed when you were merrily beginning the journey. Pretty soon, you are ankle-deep in snow, the cold wind is whipping against you, and you are wondering if this was the right thing to do at all.

If you don't have a deep foundational belief down to your core that you are right and the goal is worth the hardship, you will give up. You will decide that things were good enough on the side of the mountain where you started. You will begin to ponder what would be all that bad about just going back to the way things were.

I know this happens in the dental industry. In many cases, the dentist will get a great new idea at a seminar or conference. The doctor will begin the process of forming a goal for a new implementation at the conference. This is one of the few places where a dentist finds time think clearly, due to their constant daily barrage of requests from both patients and staff members. You see, most dentists got into the business to help people, and very few will protect their time against Time Stealers. Most dentists are just good people who want to help others. They do understand that business improvements would help their lives, but the constant drain from others makes it extremely hard for them to change anything in the workings of the office. Let's just say that they came to believe that some little change would really help them while they had some time to think clearly at the conference. That belief had better be a strong one. The reason is that the very second they get back to the office, that tidal wave of time sucking will strike. Soon, the doctor's desire to continue on his or her journey will wane if the core belief isn't as strong as it should be. All of this can be traced back to ineffectual systems the doctor put into place him- or herself. Still, those systems are there and they must be overcome. If all the time requests weren't enough of a drain on the doctor, there are other obstacles to overcome. The people around you will stand in your way too. Employees never like change. They will either overtly or covertly find ways to run this train off the tracks. Sometimes they will just do their best to swamp the doctor so that it is impossible to implement the new strategy. Sometimes they will gripe and whine about it. Sometimes they will subgroup and try to find strength in numbers to try to convince the doctor that they should just keep things the way they were. Let's not forget about the spouse of the dentist. Many times, he or she will give the dentist trouble about trying to change things as well. Like I said, nobody likes change.

If the dentist in the above example didn't *know* that the change would be for the better, there's no way he would keep going on the journey.

No wonder so many in this profession have settled into a comfortable existence with only a distant view of the mountain.

There is some light at the end of the tunnel. You must not always stand alone to face your critics forever. It is a fact of nature that people are naturally attracted to anyone who has that strong core belief in themselves and their ideas. The trick is that you have to be willing and able to stand-alone for a little while. Slowly, others will come to your aid, and it will become easier to stand firm as you have support for your ideas around you.

A good example from history would have to be from World War II. I think the prime example of core belief in a person's ideas from that war had to be Winston Churchill. For a long time, Churchill was the only person who believed that Germany was really a threat to England. Churchill was laughed at and scoffed at. Still, he continued his warnings about Hitler until almost everyone else on his island was tired of hearing them. Still he kept on. Finally, to his own dismay, Churchill's fears proved true and Britain was plunged headfirst into war. Churchill's belief didn't stop there. Now he formed another goal. His first goal had been to convince his nation that Germany was up to no good. Now that it was apparent that he had been right, Churchill had the goal to defend England and win the war. I have heard it said that he was the right man at the right place in history to lead that country. Many historians credit his will and belief as the major component in the success that England had against what seemed like a superior foe, the Third Reich.

Another example of the power of belief from the pages of history includes the famous Napoleon Bonaparte. Napoleon had been fighting in Egypt when he learned that his old rival, Austria, had taken Italy. He quickly redirected his purposes and went back to Europe. Once there, he devised an incomprehensible plan to surprise the Austrian army in the Cisalpine Republic. He was right to think this would surprise the Austrians, because almost no one would have suspected an entire army would attempt to cross the Alps. Napoleon believed that his plan would work, even if no one else did. He also had the authority to carry out his plan. On May 15, 1800, his army of forty thousand men began the crossing. One month later, the shocked Austrian army had been defeated and driven from Italy.[5] It is true that France lost many men in the battle, but the sheer audacity of the feat cemented Napoleon's legacy as a strong leader forever. A man without belief could have never pulled this off.

A more contemporary story of amazing belief would have to be that of football player Daniel Ruettiger. "Rudy," as he was called, grew up in Joliet, Illinois. He had always dreamed of playing football for the greatest college team in the nation at the time, Notre Dame. He had a few things going against him. First off, he was pretty small. His five-foot-six-inch frame with 165 pounds on it had been good enough to lead his high school team in tackles, but no one believed that he could have possibly competed in college, much less at Notre Dame. Heart and desire had gotten him a long way in high school on the football field, but his grades had suffered greatly. It turned out later that he suffered dyslexia, but that wasn't known in high school. His grades weren't good. The fact that his high school transcript was so deficient, coupled with his physical size, made his dream beyond unlikely. But, Rudy believed in himself. He managed to get himself into a college in the same town as Notre Dame, Holy Cross. His discovery of his learning disability improved his grades, but each letter of application to Notre Dame after each semester at Holy Cross was rejected. Finally, on his fourth and last try to get into his dream school, he was accepted. To have gotten this far was more than improbable. Now, the story gets even more incredible. He was a student at Notre Dame and was eligible to try out for a position on the team at a "walk-on" tryout. It occasionally does happen that someone may unexpectedly make the team from the walk-on day, but it is not a normal occurrence. Amazingly, the coaches saw the

---

5   *http://en.wikipedia.org/wiki/Bonaparte_Crossing_the_Alps*

desire and effort displayed by Rudy and granted him a spot on the scout team. That is the team that studies and runs the plays for the opposing team each week. They do this so the starters can get some experience running plays against the kind of opposing defenses and offenses they will face. Once again, it is possible that a player from the scout team might see the field in a real game, but it is highly unlikely. How Ruettiger managed to withstand all the physical and mental punishment he must have taken to get in this position, I can barely conceive. This just goes to show how this law of belief works every time it is tried, really tried. Finally, in the last game of Rudy's last year, he was granted the privilege of "dressing out" for the final home game. Dressing out is an honor, because only a few of the players on the team's roster actually get to put on the team's jersey and go onto the field and sideline for a particular game. Rudy was on the list for that day. He still had no real hopes or aspirations of getting on the field. Notre Dame was playing Georgia Tech, and they had hopes of winning the national championship. Rudy himself wouldn't have wanted to get out on the field if he wasn't the best player at a particular position. He wouldn't have wanted to hurt the team's chances. Maybe he could get out there for one play and have a chance to get an actual statistic if the team was comfortably ahead in the fourth quarter. That was still a stretch because of the strength of Georgia Tech. As all the puzzle pieces of fate fell into place, Notre Dame did have a big lead in the fourth quarter. Rudy did get into the game. Guess what? He even sacked the quarterback on one of his plays. He got his statistic. Now he would have a place in recorded history as an official player for the Notre Dame Fighting Irish forever. What a story that is. Ruettiger went on to finish his degree and still uses his amazing power of belief to achieve great things to this day.

How do you know that you have the belief you need to move forward confidently to the next chapter and the next law?

I suppose this is one of those things that only the person involved can truly look inside and say to themselves that they know they are right.

You have to look at each individual goal and test each one. Look at the goal from every aspect. Test it with the Law of the Right Mind and see if it still has merit. Make sure that you have applied all the principles we have talked about. If you have, just go for it. Think about the examples we talked about and any of the other countless inspirational stories and people you know. Form your core belief and use that strength to move forward.

If you find yourself in the position of wading up the mountain in the snowstorm, even if you had chains and weights upon your back, remember why you started this journey in the first place. Visualize the end result and why you wanted it to happen. Use your inner strength and push over that mountain. I'll promise you that after a while, the road will get easier, the path will get straighter, and the naysayers will slink off into the shadows.

How can a person cure a lack of belief?

In the rare circumstance that you find yourself not really believing that you can succeed and obtain your goal, you need some medicine. I am licensed to prescribe medicine in the United States, but I am about to prescribe something else. When I encounter those tough times where I just can't get up the energy to believe in myself, I don't simply go forward to the Law of Courage and hope for the best. No, I have to get my spirit in the right place. Now, I have to admit that I am coming from the position of being a dude. My advice may not translate well into female in this particular example. For that matter, let me go ahead and apologize to all the ladies for the references to war and sports contained in these pages. If I ever write a book called *Time Genius for Women,* I will probably need to go to sensitivity training, and I promise to get research from the best women who ever walked the planet. For now, I am subject to my own setting in life. I grew up idolizing John Wayne, Clint Eastwood, and Elvis Presley. Sorry, I can't change my stripes. I can only relate what has worked for me.

Immersion Therapy

When I am in those spots of self-doubt, I inevitably turn to motivational media. I will go re-read sections of old books and new books that I know will brighten my outlook. I listen to a motivational stretch on my MP3 player that I know always makes me feel invincible. I watch parts of old movies that really make me feel like I can do anything. And don't forget about the people you are surrounding yourselves with. A constant drumbeat of negativity will inevitably soak into your psyche. You just can't afford to waste your precious time and spirit around naysayers, naggers, or nincompoops. You may have heard the story about how eagles fly with eagles and crows fly with crows. It sounds like something rehashed from bad motivational material from the eighties, but it is the truth. I believe that a person can force their mind into the place that allows belief to come easier. When your mind is in a receptive place, it is easier to believe than if your mind is in the wrong emotional state. You can also skip ahead to the Law of Motivation if you need even more help. That chapter is at the end of the laws for a reason, but don't be afraid to read it out of order if you feel like you need it at any time. Now, it is also possible that you made a mistake in the Law of the Right Mind. If you just can't muster the belief to move forward, even after adding motivation to belief, you may have made a wrong turn in the sequence of the Right Mind. Go back and revisit that. If you are convinced that you went through that law correctly, you will find some way to get your belief going so you can move forward.

You may also need to revisit your development of your own core beliefs. If you are having trouble placing belief in your tool belt of success, your goal may be at odds with your core belief system. The core belief of your being must be in agreement with all of these laws or you won't be able to honestly move toward the achievement of your ideal goal.

I know that when I was unsure of my situation in between jobs all those years ago, I couldn't muster belief to save my life for the longest time. When I finally believed and had faith in my decision, I conquered obstacles that I would have thought impossible before I had the power of belief going for me.

P.P.S.

Perfectly Precise Summary

1.) Belief must be true and present to go forward in any goal process.
2.) When you don't believe in yourself, your own mind sabotages your progress.
3.) Amazing things can be accomplished with true belief.
4.) You must immerse yourself in the things that give you strength to believe when that belief falters.
5.) If you cannot believe after Immersion Therapy, go back to the Law of the Right Mind and rethink your goal.

Chapter 4

Law 4: Courage
You've got to fight for your right.

It is doubtful that any good new idea would ever move forward to realization if not for courage. There are all kinds of courage that any person will need to draw upon when they are trying to improve themselves or achieve something new.

> *"All men are timid on entering any fight. Whether it is the first or the last fight, all are timid. Cowards are those who let their timidity get the better of their manhood."*
>
> *"Courage is fear holding on a minute longer."*
> **—General George Patton**

Fear has been around since the beginning of time. It seems to take away the courage to act effectively. To give ourselves the courage to move forward in pursuit of our goal, we need to figure out what kinds of fears we will likely face along the way. There are a blue million of these, but the following are particularly popular.

Fear of Failure

No one wants to fail. To really try at something and fail would make public the fact that we just didn't have it in us to succeed in the first place. No one's ego is going to readily allow that opportunity to come close to happening. This starts in grade school, when we feel extreme anxiety and pressure to conform. We want to fit in, and our little brains do everything they can to try not to rock the boat. This is exacerbated by the fact that children are many times cruel to each other. Kids are frequently unreceptive to ideas and things that are "different." This will enact a mechanism deep within our young psyche that tries its best to conform and receive the acceptance of the other kids. Fear of failure plays a role in human activity all the way from the highest achievement motivation to the accomplishment of the smallest project. Therefore, we must consider it when trying to accomplish any improvement in time or ourselves. This fear resides mostly in the part of us that has to convince ourselves that our goal is worthy. Even though we may fear the words and thoughts of others, this is only a reflection of the fear we have of inadequacy. We may have created a really impressive façade for others to see. We may have fooled them into believing that façade to be the real us. We may have even convinced our outer self that this façade is real. It may be technically real for all intents and purposes. But we know the truth. Ultimately, we know which parts of our public figure are true and which ones are false or exaggerated. I think our subconscious self always maintains this knowledge, even if it is suppressed and hidden from our outer self. It is this honest assessment by our inner self that fuels the fear of failure. When our outward self and inner self become more in tune with each other through honest reflection and consideration, the fear of failure will begin to lose power and fade away. This is not to say that we will be able to do anything our minds can imagine. Of course we will always have some strength and some limitations. We will become more honest with ourselves about our skill sets. This will allow us to make better choices about our role in the sequence of events of any goal implementation.

Fear of Rejection

This fear is also housed in our brains, but definitely involves other people more than the fear of failure. In this case, we are not so much concerned with what we will be able to accomplish. We are concerned about what others will think about us. Of course, this is always an exaggerated fear. Most people in the world are so concerned about their own affairs that they really don't care about anything we are doing.

I know from personal experience that this is an all-too-real fear. As I look into my own life, I know that the fear of failure stopped me from accomplishing many things in life. Why the adolescent boy or girl thinks that the world revolves around them so much, I have no idea. It is still a factual statement that they do think that. Almost every action is considered and measured against what their friends or peer group will say or think about that action. I was pretty good at getting straight As in school. I was the one who ruined the curve for the rest of the class. When I was very young, I took a lot of pleasure in getting those straight 100s. Sometime in puberty, I figured out that this was making my friends mad. In an effort to fit in, I intentionally hid the fact that I was getting those good grades throughout high school. The damage was done, and some of those kids never forgave me for scoring high and rubbing their noses in it, but I still tried. I would score a 100 on a test and then proceed to act like the test was so hard that I probably flunked it. I would pretend that I didn't know what the answers were as we discussed it in the halls afterward. All the while, my true inner self was screaming the answer. It got to a point where I would cut up in class, talk, maybe toss a paper to someone, or skip class just to attempt to cover up the fact that I was the curve buster. I am so glad that I didn't take it to the next level, actual flunking. Still, I should have had the inner strength to say, "This is what I am. I make good grades. Sorry." Instead, I tried to be something I wasn't. My inner self and outer self were all screwed up. I don't think they spoke much during high school or junior high.

Let's talk about the opposite sex. I don't know much about how girls think. (Just ask my wife.) I do know a lot about how I got along with girls. The actual interaction with the girls was at a minimum, mostly due to this fear of failure. What did I fear? If I can remember this correctly, I feared that the girl would turn me down and laugh at me if I asked her out. It took months and years of wanting to ask out any particular girl for me to work up the courage to ask one of them out. I was so fearful, my insides would turn upside down and I found breathing very difficult. I'm sure that my red-faced, sweaty presentation certainly added to my chances of actual failure. This led to more rejection. More rejection led to the belief that more rejection was to come. All of this snowballed, and it made each subsequent attempt that much harder. I'll just come out and say that my all-time batting average for success in asking girls out was below the Mendoza line. For all of you non-baseball trivia fans that is a very, very low success percentage. Fear of failure kept the percentage low because it planted the doubt in my mind to the extent that I could never believe that I would succeed. It also kept me from trying more than I did. Sometimes the fear was so great that I just gave up without a try.

Fear of failure has reared its ugly head for most of my life. I'll bet it has followed you around too. In business, I have encountered this in lots of variations. One of the most common is the fear to try something new in business. You will probably need to be most conscious of this as you work your way through this book and try to implement your goals. This fear will pop up when you first hear about some great new idea. You may have heard how some other peer has used a technique to great advantage. You may have seen a wonderful thing in another industry and figured out how you can apply it to your industry. Either way, you will be stepping out of the box, either in your industry as a whole or in the context of your own status quo. Your fears may be that you will flop if you try this new thing. You may fear that your friends will laugh at you. You may fear that your staff will think that you are not a good leader if you fail. You may fear what your spouse will think if you go out on this limb and it breaks under you. Most of the time, these fears are unfounded, but the fact that we fear the failure makes this a very real problem. We must fight through this in order to move on to the next step in our implementation adventure.

Fear of Loss

This fear will crop up in the business world more than most fears. We will have to overcome this fear to succeed at any objective that has the potential of greatness. Let's consider the already-established practitioner or businessman. This person probably has a nice place of business, a little money in the bank, and a smooth operation overall. If this person aspires to a high goal, they will have to risk some of their entire storehouse of goods to chase this dream. The fear of loss will keep a lot of competent people on the sidelines. They will weigh the reward against the risk required, and they may just decide to keep things the way they are. In fact, I would say that most people will decide to stay where they are, even if they have an honest-to-goodness great idea and the risks are manageable. Why would they do this? The fear of loss can be the only explanation. This fear will make otherwise courageous achievers shrink back from some big challenge.

This is one reason it is such a hindrance in the pursuit of really big wealth for a person to have a comfortable living. The person who has plenty of money in the bank will find it very hard to risk that money to chase even bigger money. The newbie who hasn't got two plug nickels to rub together doesn't have the same amount of skin in the game. They can more freely risk everything, because it's not that much to begin with. Also, they can lose everything and get back to their starting point rather quickly. The established and successful businessman who took years to create some minor wealth will find it exceedingly harder to risk it all.

I think I speak from some level of experience here. The fear of loss has definitely kept me on the sidelines at times in my own life. Several years ago, my best friend called me over the Christmas holidays. For those of you reading this who are not dentists, I will fill you in on a little inside baseball. Dentists are usually too stressed out during the year to think of much besides their practices and families. Those who can manage to think outside that box usually succeed big time. Christmas is traditionally a time when a dentist can take off a week or so and get away from the daily grind. That's when I do my own best thinking and develop my goals for the next year. Anyway, my friend calls me up and says he just read *Rich Dad, Poor Dad.* He and I had always said that we wanted to get into business together someday and do a joint venture outside of dentistry. He said that he wanted to start building a real-estate empire and he wanted me to be his partner. Now, I never considered real estate. I don't own much real estate, and I never really wanted to. It doesn't appeal to me in the slightest. I did owe it to him to read the book. I did. It was a good book, and I believed that we could probably follow the guidelines in that book and succeed, much like you can follow the laws in this book and succeed. Still, I had a healthy dose of fear of loss going on inside my gut. I had just begun to build back my bank accounts after a catastrophic event in my own life, and I just didn't want to risk it right then. I told him that I just didn't want to get into a lot of debt at that time. He was disappointed, but he went ahead, slew his own demons, and invested heavily in his local real estate. Even with the market collapse, he has managed not only to do well but thrive in this tough real estate economy.

He asked me for a while if I wanted in on one of his new deals. I always decline. He has stopped asking so much these days. I did offer him a partnership in my consulting business a couple of years ago, and he declined, so maybe we're even. I still hope we can do something together before we get too old.

> "It is easy to be brave from a safe distance." –**Aesop**

Overcoming Fear

What was the catastrophic event I mentioned in the above section? What event changed my life and forced me to overcome all the above fears and more? Well, I'll tell you.

I had been an honor student throughout my education until I got to dental school. Once there, I had worked out a deal to go into business with my childhood dentist as an associate, with hopes to one day buy the practice from him. I thought this was such an amazing deal that I started to question my desire to be at the head of my dental school class. Also, my competition was much greater than in the past. I was going to have to really study to get into the top ten. I decided (no excuse, just fact) to "dog" it a little bit. This means that I didn't study as hard as I could have. I knew I was set up for life when I got out of school, so I didn't get the grades I could have. I didn't care about anything but simply passing the courses for the first time in my life. This was loads of fun. I finally found out what most of my friends up to this point already knew: school is more fun when you aren't studying all the time.

I got out of dental school and went into practice with my childhood dentist. Things started out well enough. As time went forward, I started to get a sick feeling in my stomach, and I began to think that things might not work out between us. This shouldn't shock anyone, but I had never considered the possibility of a failed business relationship with this guy. About a month before my contract ran out, my wife came to me and told me that she was pregnant. Whoa. Now I am sick to death about my future in this practice and my wife's with child. The pressure began to build. Over the next couple of weeks, my relationship with the other dentist rapidly disintegrated. It became obvious that I was going to have to move on. Now I was one year out of school and in serious debt. My wife was pregnant and wasn't about to leave her mother and family behind at this point in her life. I couldn't get a job anywhere near my hometown, due to lack of population and the number of other dentists. I had only two choices: I had to either crawl back to my childhood dentist and beg for a job or build my own practice from scratch.

I remember the night that I made the decision. I was sitting on the floor of the kitchen in our starter home. I had just gotten off the phone with yet another local dentist who wouldn't hire me as an associate. My wife was asleep in the bedroom, in between bouts of stomach queasiness associated with the pregnancy. I was sicker than anyone. I was feeling all those fears building up inside. Suddenly, all my thoughts came together, and I made my decision. I decided that whatever it took, I was going to build my own place and succeed. I didn't care if it took eighty-hour weeks and odd jobs; I was going to do it, come heck or high water. I cannot describe the power and exhilaration that came from that lone moment of decision. It was as if a torch was lit deep inside my psyche. I couldn't make myself go to bed. I stayed up all night, sketching ideas and drawings onto pieces of paper. The next day, I started searching for a physical location to house this baby practice. I found an old home that hadn't been lived in for quite a while. It took three months of fourteen-hour days, but ninety days after I left my other job, I opened Griffin Dental, P.A. I still had enough juice left in me to go on to become the youngest dentist at that time to be awarded a fellowship in the Academy of General Dentistry at age twenty-nine. That is an earned award for competency in varied disciplines of dentistry. I guess I applied all the energy I wasted in dental school to attaining this high award. I just had to do it to prove to myself that I hadn't lost the touch.

In the business world, you will no doubt face all the fears we have talked about. True courage is not the lack of acknowledging those fears. True courage is facing them, knowing that they will exact their pound of flesh. True courage is standing fast when those fears beat against you and remaining standing until they subside. Trust me, they will subside.

P.P.S.

Perfectly Precise Summary

1.) Fear is a natural emotion in people.

2.) You must understand that emotion in its different manifestations to overcome it.

3.) Courage can be displayed by anyone.

Chapter 5

Law 5: Visual Learning
The Show Me State of Mind

There exists a bridge between the first few thought laws and the action laws that follow. Visual learning becomes the first practical step from taking your new goal from your mind and putting it into the physical world. Here, I hope to show how the observation of others strengthens your belief and places that belief into action. Once you have come to believe in your idea and have pushed past the fears to bring it forward, you need some little something to solidify your beliefs. This is necessary to firm up your convictions before you move forward. Another way to think about this is to consider the psychological concept of social proof. My concept of social proof is that human beings have always had an instinct deep inside them that takes over in certain situations. Social proof would be stimulated when someone is unsure of the proper behavior they should show in a particular setting. In our example, social proof is very important because it allows someone to feel confident that they have believed in something correctly. Since belief and courage have to be solidified before a person can move forward with any achievement, our minds need proof that they are on the right track if they are going to get the results they want.

Let me recount an example from my own life. A few years ago, I was traveling to Atlanta with some friends when we heard an audio CD from a famously productive dentist in Florida. One of the problems that all of us in the vehicle were experiencing at the time was a general lack of treatment acceptance by our patients. The reason given by most of the patients was always that the cost of the preferred treatment was too high. To put it simply, more and more patients were telling us to "pull it," instead of "fix it." "Fixing it" was obviously more expensive and, thus, the problem. We would have loved to have "fixed" everyone's teeth at a price they could afford, but we couldn't solve the problem of supply in our practices. There was only so much time and doctor to go around. The voice on the CD seemed to come right out of the console and slap me in the face. It was then and there that I had an "a-ha" moment about how I could stretch the amount of doctor available in the office and lower prices so that more people could choose optimal care for their teeth.

All that weekend, I schemed and set up my ideal goals for this undertaking. Back then, our hotel didn't even have wireless Internet, so I had to spend some time researching my goals in the business office downstairs. After a while, I had the concrete goals established. Then I had to go through the process of the Right Mind to make sure my goals made sense. I quizzed my friends all that weekend about the specifics of my plan. I made some changes to the goals and finally I had something that made sense to everyone. Next, I did some serious soul searching and tested my theories against my own true core beliefs. They seemed congruent. I actually believed that I could cut the cycle time of my procedures down while maintaining quality. Courage was the next obstacle. No dentist wants to be thought of—by patients or other dentists—as one who rushes through procedures. I knew I would face some critics, because most dentists in the world believe that the longer, more complicated, and more expensive a procedure, the better it is. This thinking is deeply ingrained in dental school and permeates our community. Many also look down their noses at any dentist who charges a low or even a moderate fee for procedures. I know the dentists of whom I was scared were probably in the minority, but those are usually the vocal ones. That makes it seem like the whole world of dentists is against you when their disapproval becomes obvious.

Having overcome my fears and found my courage to proceed, I made plans to visit the dentist from the CD in Florida. Actually, I called his office and spoke to him. I'll share a funny story with you. I had decided to go down there with all my close dentist buddies. I thought we were really on to something, and I wanted us all to share in the educational experience of seeing his office systems in person. There were eight of us in all. I was the spokesman for the group. On the phone with this brilliant doctor, I told him that we had heard him on audio and wanted to witness him in action. He said that he had so many requests for this that he charged $5,000 for each group to visit. Here's where I don't remember who miscommunicated with whom. Rest assured that there was a miscommunication. He said that he would be glad for us to come and transferred me to his assistant to work out the details. I spoke to her about dates, and we set up the visit. She asked me for the names of all the attendees and told me how to send them the money. I sent a check for five grand. I was making these plans about two months before our scheduled visit. During the next two months, I spoke to the dentist's assistant a few times. Things seemed to be running on schedule. In the interim, I had told all my friends, seven in all, that we could split up the $5,000 fee among us. Everyone sent me their portion and made their plans. For a health care provider, this involves not only the usual airfare and hotel charges, but patient rescheduling and coverage for clinics. This can be quite an undertaking and requires a good bit of work to get everything ironed out perfectly. Anyway, we were all set to come down when the assistant called. She said, "Dr. Griffin, we were just wondering when your friends would be sending their money for the in-office observation day." Pause. Do what? I politely asked her what she meant. She said that the cost for each doctor was $5,000, and since we had eight total doctors coming, they were expecting another $35,000 for the visit. Awkward silence on my end. When I finally gathered my own teeth off the floor and came to my senses enough to speak, I told her that I had understood that the cost for the entire group was to be 5,000 total dollars. Awkward silence on her end. She said that the fee was always per doctor and that it was her responsibility to take care of these days for the doctor since he was so busy. Now we both had a problem. The doctor must have quoted me that fee because either I hadn't told him that our group was all doctors or he hadn't realized that we were all doctors when he quoted me the fee. Also, his assistant hadn't caught the mistake and made the total fee clear even though she knew we were all doctors. What were we to do?

The only thing to do was to go to the doctor and tell him the misunderstanding. I hoped he would understand about all the trouble the other doctors had undertaken to get down there and take pity on us. However, I couldn't remember if I had been clear, and it certainly would have been in his power to tell us to cough up the extra dough or not come at all. Thankfully, the doctor was understanding and he let us come on down for the original $5,000. Looking back, it would have been a bargain if I had paid the entire 40,000 bucks myself if you consider all the wonderful things I learned there. It was as if watching this operator work turned my semi-solid mass of a plan into the hardest granite on the planet. Seeing the procedures and protocols carried out by another dentist solidified my belief. When my brain quit buzzing and the dust cleared, my ideal goal was completely mature and I was ready to launch it into action. If I hadn't seen this dentist operate, I might have gone into the next phase of battle half-heartedly. As it was, I had the backbone I needed to move forward.

I have used this law to my advantage multiple times in my dental practice. Each time I come upon a new idea, concept, or procedure I want to incorporate, I find a practitioner somewhere in the world who is already doing it. Note: If someone else is doing something you want to do, it is probably possible. I know this is common sense (see Right Mind Law), but I can assure you that you will find plenty of naysayers whenever you try something new.

Each time I visit a dentist to learn, I solve some problem. The only time I came away disappointed was when I visited a dentist who had twenty offices throughout the country. You see, at one time I had toyed with the idea of expanding my offices and branching out into satellites. I had gotten the idea past the beginning laws and was ready for the Visual Learning step. What I saw was more than I had bargained for. The dentist was very wealthy, but he worked much harder than I would ever want to work. In fact, he said that if you liked hobbies or not working on weekends, this was not for you. I believed him when I saw all the checklists he filled out each day. It was not a complete failure, though. After seeing all this with my own two eyes, I knew I didn't want to pursue this idea any further. I saw that it was possible, but that it would require more time than I was ready to invest.

This is something you will encounter as you take different ideas through these twelve laws. You will get up to a certain law and realize that there was a flaw or underestimation somewhere in your plan. This is a good thing. No one can get everything perfect when they first birth a plan from their mind. If that was the case, there would be a group of people sitting around somewhere just thinking stuff up and telling us regular people what to do. That ain't the case. This is the real world, and here we work out solutions to problems through trial and error. Every now and then, we will spend a good bit of time and effort trying to produce a certain effect, only to find that we have made a mistake along the way. That is when we go back in our protocol to find out where we made our error. Then, we have the choice to both correct that miscalculation and test the goal through the same process that found the error, or start over with another goal in mind. Visual Learning will catch a lot of these miscalculations before you get too far along the wrong path. Just make sure you don't skip ahead or you may end up investing so much time and effort that you cannot bear the thought of scrapping the project. That's when you get into trouble.

> *"People seldom improve when they have no other model but themselves to copy after".* – **Oliver Goldsmith**

Another good example applying Visual Learning occurs every day in the world of information. Let's say someone buys into the idea that they want to learn how to do something. What they are really buying into is the end product. Just knowing that they want to do something is nowhere near half the battle. There are many steps that will hang up a new learner as they enter a domain in which they have no experience. The trend toward teaching videos and tutorials is addressing this issue. Now it is common for someone to get access to videos that walk them through the little processes step by step. The fact that the student can see another human being performing the exact actions that they want to learn is invaluable. There is no way that written or spoken instructions can match the power of the visual education. Of course, I personally like to soak in all three when I am learning; I think the video is the most powerful. Maybe it is due to my background with labs in college. You can imagine that just about every biology, physics, or chemistry course I took had a laboratory course attached to it. At the time, I didn't appreciate the labs. I thought that I could learn everything in the class or in the book. I thought these three-hour classes were a waste of time. Boy, was I wrong. I'm sure I got as much or more out of these workshop-type courses as the lectures themselves. Even though I didn't like it at the time, I was building my understanding of visual learning as a vital component of learning any new activity.

Let me give you some tips when you get your opportunity to apply Visual Learning. Remember, your job is to observe, take notes, then replicate what you see as it applies to your own ideal goal. Of course, as we have already stated, you may observe, take notes, and decide this is not for you.

Tip 1: Pay attention to the small details. It is going to be easy to become overwhelmed when you encounter someone who is doing great things that you want to achieve yourself. The danger in this is that you will come away from your visit with a feeling that the teacher was totally awesome, but with no real action steps to perform.

Tip 2: Video record the encounter if permissible. The teacher will not always allow this, and for good reason. In the case of a professional, there may be some privacy issues to consider. However, if you are allowed to record these visits, take full advantage. You will be able to sit down later and map out every little detail. Many times, the operator doesn't even realize all the little cool things they are doing to make themselves successful. The video will give you the chance to break it down just like a sports coach. You can do the same thing with a video on the Internet or on DVD if that is the way you are going to approach the Law of Visual Learning.

Tip 3: Take notes of all the high points. If you can't videotape it, you should do your best to get all the little details too. However, don't fall into the trap of trying to write so many notes that you miss important points. This is a real danger because it is nearly impossible to write as fast as the teacher can perform the action. An alternative would be to use a voice recorder to speak your notes into. This will save lots of time, and you can go over them slowly later. Once again, be conscious of privacy concerns and get permission from the teacher if you will be capturing their voice.

Tip 4: Form an action plan before you leave. You need to at least go over your notes enough to form an action plan before you leave the site of the experience. This doesn't have to be completely detailed, and you can add to it later, but get a general plan of action down on paper before you physically leave the area. While your brain is spinning out good ideas, you may as well take advantage of the situation.

Besides just getting you ready to take your goal from thought to action, the Law of Visual Learning will usually spin off good ideas that you haven't even considered. Just log these away if you aren't ready to work on them right now. There will come a time when those new ideas will be worth their weight in gold.

If your ideal goal has passed muster in the Visual Learning phase, now we're ready to implement.

P.P.S.

Perfectly Precise Summary
1.) You can learn some things by observing a master that you cannot pick up on any other way.
2.) Choose a few masters you want to observe.
3.) Get permission to watch them.
4.) If you can't get that, find a way to get some video of a master at work.

Chapter 6

Law 6: Operations
"What are we talking about ... practice?"

I'm sure that any basketball fan will recognize the chapter subheading as a quote from NBA star Allen Iverson. At the time, Iverson was being disciplined by his coach, Larry Brown of the Philadelphia 76ers, for not practicing before a game. He made the statement famous when he used the word *practice* about twenty times in a two-minute press conference. It was funny because every ex-athlete has the importance of practice beaten into their head at an early age. You always hear coaches say things like, "You play games like you practice." You hear that "practice makes perfect." All these things have been repeated so much in our culture that they have become cliché. I am afraid that this designation has taken away some of the wisdom contained in those words. It is true that practice *makes* perfect. It is true that good practice leads to good games. It is not the other way around. You can't simply go out and play a game and expect to perform at your tip-top best level of excellence without practice beforehand. Why do you think that all coaches have one last practice before each game where they try to make the surroundings and atmosphere as close to game time scenario as possible? It is because they want the players to refine their efforts from practice and translate them into a performance that shows their abilities at their best. Another wise classic statement is that "you just can't throw your shoes onto the court and expect to win." The point of that one is that some teams think they are so good that all they have to do is show up to a game and play without really trying hard at that game or practicing hard beforehand. Practice is where the gold standard of any final operation begins to gain a foothold. Practice is where ideas are tested in the line of fire. Some ideas survive this test and others are mortally wounded. It is the place for trial and error. Don't be alarmed if you experience more errors than successes here. As a dentist, I know why they call any medical operation a "practice." It's not because every situation is always the same and has only one solution. It is because every situation is different, and most require a lot of trial and error to get a workable solution. You just have to trust your idea and jump in with both feet first.

> *"I have not failed 700 times. I have not failed once. I have succeeded in proving that those 700 ways will not work. When I have eliminated the ways that will not work, I will find the way that will work."*
> —**Thomas Edison.**[6]

Paralysis by Analysis

Some people are blessed with the ability to take any idea and run headlong into any danger whatsoever to test its validity. These are the people who become famous. Oftentimes, their stories will also include a period of time when they risked and lost it all in pursuit of their dream. It is in their nature to act first and question later. Sometimes this is a serious advantage, such as in the pursuit of wealth or poverty. Either one can be gained readily by charging into a situation without properly surveying the situation. I don't think the majority of folks out there are graced with this genetic propensity. Most of us are very cautious about diving into any decision. If you are reading this book,

---

6   *http://en.wikiquote.org/wiki/Thomas_Edison*

you are probably either at a high level in business, an entrepreneur, or an entrepreneur wannabe. This means that you already have long ago passed the threshold of decision-making that keeps the average soccer mom on the car lot for hour upon hour when choosing the new minivan. Just by reaching this section of this book, you have already displayed enough action to keep reading a book that is challenging the way you do things. All this bodes well for you. Beware: *there is still time to screw this thing up.*

You may be a very technical, engineer type of a person. If so, you will want to get your hands on all the available data and research before plunging into any new activity. That's just for any old thing, much less a major goal in your life. I went to Mississippi State to become an engineer, and I lived with engineers the whole time I was there. I'll assure you that they suffer from the "paralysis by analysis" malady to an extreme extent. Now, this is not to say that a person with this affliction isn't being smart about their actions. It just means that they will run trials in their heads over and over until they think they have gotten it right. They will purposely avoid putting anything into concrete action until they feel their chances of success are greatly enhanced. The truth of the matter is that these people might very well have a better batting average when they actually pull the trigger on a project. However, I have always joked with my friends who show a predilection for "paralysis." I say that I may make a lot of wrong decisions, but I will have made ten right ones before they make any at all. I always say this tongue in cheek, but deep down, I truly believe it. I think it is much better to get "off the pot" and go with something that is not "perfect" than to nitpick an idea until it bleeds to death from inaction. Worse yet, sometimes these people will have a great idea early on, but their inaction will cause them delay until someone else brings their version of the same idea to market. It may very well be that the "paralysis" victim had the better idea and had it first. You still can't compete and win consistently with someone who is willing to throw caution to the wind and charge into the marketplace with their idea. Like

I said before, sometimes those people charge straight into a bayonet, but sometimes they ride to glory.

Good Records and Measurement

Hopefully, I have convinced you to get off your backside and get into the game with whatever idea or goal you have brought this far into the Twelve Laws. Now, it is time to get a little more technical. I know that up until now, we have enjoyed a lot of theory and discussion. Those are the fun parts of any new launch of ideas. There are some good old-fashioned principles that must be followed if we want to really experience success. How can we know if we are becoming successful with the implementation of our goal into the real world? We have to measure our results.

When a young child is trying to implement the goal of learning about their environment, they may come across some chances for trial and error. If that child touches a hot surface, the result seared into the brain is both reliable and long lasting. That hot surface also gives immediate feedback that the child can use. To top it off, many times, nature gives the child a physical and perennial reminder of the action of touching the surface: a scar. We should always be looking to nature and the entire physical world for education. The world gives us measurements and records that are both immediate and permanent. These lessons can reach us and other inhabitants through all of modes: auditory, visual, emotional, etc. The child in the above example is very unlikely to burn himself very readily in the future because of the practice and readjustment that was experienced. The child experienced trial and error. In this case, the penalty for touching the hot surface was severe enough to cause a change of course after the data was entered deeply into the child's brain.

The main objective of records must be to increase our chance of success by showing us the results of different variations of our ideal goal. We want to quantify the situation and give ourselves more rock-solid information than is readily available through our human senses (or perceptions of what is going on).

The purpose of these records is to master time. With these records, we can command the past to come back to life. We can look into the future and predict outcomes with a high degree of success. We can check our work inside the other laws to make sure we made the correct assumptions and decisions. We can also correct mistakes or wrong turns along the way as we interpret our findings with these records. These same records will give us our best chance of ultimate success as we move forward.

Records are anything that gives information. Men have often tried to create records that could be passed down. Throughout history, records have been important. Good records can memorialize a tribe or people far longer than they can physically exist on Earth. Records allow us to reach back into the distant past and learn from our ancestors' mistakes. The problem has not come as one of man's indecision about making records. Rather, it has been a problem of how to secure these records once they are made. It is certainly a shame that some ancient cultures didn't take the time to develop more detailed or long-lasting records about themselves. I have no doubt that the technology created by many ancient cultures would shock and surprise the average twenty-first centurion. We like to believe that other past civilizations' accomplishments pale in comparison. I don't believe that to be the case. In America, we certainly know more about the ancient Egyptian culture than we know about our more closely related kinfolk, the Europeans. We surely know very little about our own Native Americans. I had the fortune to grow up on a farm that had obviously been inhabited by Native Americans in large numbers at one time. Every year, when we broke the ground to plant a new year's crops, we found lots of arrowheads and spear points. A fun activity from my childhood was spending countless hours with other members of my family, walking around the freshly plowed ground, staring at the dirt. If we were lucky, we would see a tiny gleam of a colored rock. Upon closer examination, most colored rocks would turn out to have been used by Native Americans in some form or fashion. One year, we invited a college history professor to hunt these rocks with us. When we found the first ones, he informed us that these types of flint rocks far predated the arrowheads used by the Chickasaw and Choctaw tribes of near history for my area. He said that very little was known about these tribes that inhabited the lands more than a few hundred years ago. One of the reasons we don't know more about these people is that they left behind hardly anything in the way of written records. The Egyptians did a good job of permanent record keeping, and that's why we know so much of them today. Who knows what great histories we would be privileged to learn if not for the tragedy at the great library in Alexandria so many years ago?

Hopefully, our modern culture with pictures, audio and video recordings, and computers will allow us to be better understood by our progeny than our ancestors are by us.

To qualify as "helpful permanent records," two qualities must be present:

1. The records must be readily available.

2. The records must be accurate.

That is a plain and simple system, yet measurement and record keeping are sadly lacking at even some very successful enterprises. In many of the great conglomerated super-companies of today, one doesn't know which fact is more amazing. Is it the lack of quickly accessible and accurate records, or the overabundance of useless data, measurements, and records there? All of which were probably painstakingly gathered and tabulated by a highly paid accountant or at least someone who added tremendously to the company's overhead. In behemoth companies, duplication runs rampant. Data of very little value can quickly accumulate like a midnight snowfall. The problem only increases if the data is not properly manipulated to tell the owners or bosses anything of value. Most big companies (and a few little ones) let this snowfall of information go unused until it turns into a full-sized snow bank from under which no one wants to dig out the truth. This certainly doesn't help the research or measurements more readily available, whether they were correct or not. Who can really blame the underling clerk toiling away in their dungeon of an office? They work away at their monotonous jobs, compiling old and new data that no one actually looks at for the most part. This kind of inefficiency eats away at a company's profitability, and ultimately will be the death of it, even if it takes many moons to come to fruition.

We cannot allow this to happen to our data. We must be fiercely protective of it. The measurements and data we derive from our experiment with this law is going to be the compass that leads us toward the correct next step. We must carefully capture the data. I like to use the analogy of fishing for bass versus fishing for crappie. Both these game fish are abundant in the Southern freshwaters in which I fish. Bass have extremely strong jaws with lots of little teeth. The teeth aren't big enough to cut you badly, but after a long day of catching this variety, you will have a raw thumb from detaching these fish from your hook. The bass's mouth is so strong that you can really jerk back and set the hook into it. You know that if that hook engages, the fish will have no option other than to be reeled in toward your rod. On the other hand, a crappie has a very delicate mouth. Not only can you not be as aggressive in setting your hook with a crappie, you have to exercise extra caution when boating these fish. If you are too rough with the fish when pulling them from the water, the hook will literally rip the fish's mouth and the crappie will get away. I view measurement recording in much the same way. I believe that you have to be as precise and careful as you possibly can when collecting data, especially if that data will determine your future paths. If we have very accurate data and we have instant access to it, we are set to make a good decision and move on to the next phase of our implantation journey.

In my own industry, I was presented with the need to know how long it was actually taking my office to perform common procedures on patients every day. We needed to know this in order to make decisions based on staffing and equipment purchases. We needed to know whether or not we were being as efficient as possible. We also wanted to know if our times for these procedures could be improved to the point that we could comfortably squeeze in a few more patients each day. I sat down and came up with a spreadsheet that we used to determine just how efficient we actually were. I called it the "turnover tracker." It got its name from the concept of turnover in the dental office. No, I wasn't talking about the kind of turnover where you fire someone. I was talking about turnover in the way that runners and sprinters talk about turnover. It is the number of steps you take each second. I extrapolated that out to mean in our dental office, we wanted to know the number of steps (procedures) we could perform in a given period of time. You can look at the example of the Turnover Tracker on the next page and see that it contains all the pertinent information that we needed to make those decisions about the direction our clinic would go.

You can use a spreadsheet like this one to develop some record keeping for your own business. You don't have to be a dentist. It is highly likely that you have some processes that could stand a little time improvement. If that is your goal, when you get to this law, just fill in the spreadsheet with applicable data headings and head out. Start measuring and you will find out exactly where you are and where you need to go. How could you ever expect to know where you need to go if you don't know where you have been?

Time Genius

TURNOVER TRACKER

	PT.	PROC.	START TIME	TOOTH # (S)	ASST.	ROOM #	RESET TIME	ANEST. TIME	DOCTOR PROC. TIME	NON-DOC PROC. TIME	TOTAL TIME
1											
2											
3											
4											
5											
6											
7											
8											
9											
10											
11											
12											
13											
14											
15											
16											
17											
18											
19											
20											
21											
22											
23											
24											
25											

P.P.S.

Perfectly Precise Summary

1.) We have to actually get into action at some point, just jump in and do it!

2.) This law requires physical action.

3.) Records are vitally important in the achievement of a goal.

4.) Save these records for your permanent record of the goal achievement. You can use the records in the reference section of your standard operating procedure manual later.

Chapter 7

Law 7: Logistics
Your Own Personal Traffic Controller

The definition of logistics I like best is the precise scheduling and organization of any complex problem or process. The attainment of a goal or the manifestation of an idea into a workable solution qualifies, I think. You will note that I didn't say "any large problem or process. " I have found that size certainly doesn't matter. Complexity can be found in most anything worth doing, large or small. You see, it is easy to plan out and execute when the task is extraordinarily simple. It is quite different to do the same when there are many moving parts. Most of the time, it is the case that not only do the individual parts of any plan move, but the moving parts have moving parts. That is why the mind maps are so important in organizing the process into a manageable situation.

You may notice that I placed this law after the law of operations. This would seem out of order at first glance. No, it is not. Let me explain: As you read in the previous chapter, it is of utmost importance that a person finds a way to move from the thinker stage to the doer stage. Nothing has ever been accomplished of value by someone sitting around and thinking about solving a problem. All the good ideas come from people who charge in and perform, and then correct their mistakes and retry. That is why the operations must come first. This will give the person good feedback and show which failures to improve. Then, these mid-course corrections can be brought to the table to form logistics. Having had actual experience included, the plan will be all the better in the end.

Of course, never underestimate the difficulty in managing logistics. Sir Francis Galton, the noted anthropologist of the last century, talked about the difficulties a certain tribe in Southern Africa had in keeping a schedule while driving their oxen. This tribe has presumably done this task every day for hundreds of years and yet they still have a problem. It seems that the greatest risk to one of these herd drives is attack by lions. The lions always attack from the outside of the main pack. They mainly focus on the oxen out front or independently behind. The ox that stays in the middle of the pack is usually not attacked. So, through many generations, the more independent bulls and cows have been naturally selected out of the herd. Since oxen need leaders in the herd to follow, the tribe had to go to considerable lengths. They had to select and train calves they thought capable of walking ahead and leading the other herd members. I'm sure you feel their pain if you manage anything other than just yourself. Many days, it would be enough to just manage you, indeed.

Once upon a time in America, we owned a marvel of the entire world. The railroad system of the early twentieth century was truly a spectacle of modern engineering to be gawked at. It may be hard for any remaining generations of Americans to believe, but the train system was once the very best way to travel, ship, or get anything from point A to point B. Of course, times change and no one would consider themselves lucky to arrive at point B within twelve hours of the schedule time. That was not always the case. At the time, every hotel and general store had racks that were filled with railroad timetables. They were placed there by the ton each month to show the very minute in exact time over the next several weeks when every single passenger train in the United States was scheduled to reach every single station. These amazing schedules were only the abridged versions for consumption of the general public and for purposes of showing passenger trains. The employees of the railroad were given timetables that were much more detailed. This complete version covered all the passenger trains, but also covered all freight trains and special trains. The rules of operation contained in them were frighteningly detailed. The level of accuracy attained by this one industry at that time in American history showed logistics that were on par with most of the complexities of nature that one can imagine. It was said that their dispatching was almost equal to the universal movements of stars in the sky. Let us consider the lines of track between New York and Chicago, a very highly traveled route of the day. Almost a thousand miles of track stretched between the two cities. Every switch, grade, curve, and sign was known. Signal towers and stations lined the way. The machine that the railroad used to traverse this distance in precise time was a steam locomotive that used that pressure to transmit 400 horsepower to the metal rail by way of a quarter-inch contact point between the wheel of the behemoth and the perfectly smooth rail. Each one of these massive machines would derive its energy from coal and water. The train would run at about sixty miles per hour with either seventy-two or eighty-four wheel axles under the train running true in its box in complete synchronization. Every element of the operation and schedule—the track, the cross ties, all the equipment, and the men—had to be in perfect working order all the time. I know that we now have super trains in the world that go hundreds of miles per hour, but this was the early 1900s, folks. Think of the technology with which they had to work.

Considering all the above conditions, the railroad companies made out their schedules. They allowed for all the multiple variables on the eighteen-hour trip from New York to Chicago ... and the train left the station.

The dispatchers issued orders to the conductor and to the signalmen. The train was under the physical control of the engineer, who was in subjection to the orders of the conductor, but it was the dispatcher who held the real control of the train in the palm of his hand. The dispatcher watched closely the minute details and kept in touch with all of this by messenger and telephone. Every tiny town with a depot knew when the train would stop. Every signalman knew when the train would pass. It was a marvel of human skill excellence in logistics. All Americans should be proud that we once held the distinction of mastery in industry, even if for such a short while.

In my own industry of dentistry, I have looked at the logistics of many and varied aspects of the practice to try to implement new ideas or improve old ones. One of the problems that has always cropped up was the inability to see patients the entire time I was at the office. I, along with almost every dentist out there, would have days where I would work hard for a while, then be left sitting in my office, playing on the computer or shuffling through paperwork instead of treating people. It was my opinion that if I was going to spend my day away from my family and work, I should at least be seeing patients the entire time I was present. I came up with a theory that I called the 3-Day Dentist theory. I believed that if I could properly devise a system of routing myself and my patients properly throughout the office, just like a train dispatcher, I could easily see more patients in three days a week than I could in four or five. Of course, I could have easily just dropped back to three days a week and continued on in my inefficient ways, but I wanted to still be a contributor to my community. I also wanted to keep my income at the same level as it had been when I worked a full week. I ran my theory through the Twelve Laws sequence, and one of the systems that came out of the process was the inclusion of the route board. This is simply a white dry-erase board that hangs in my office in a central location. That board hosts all the information about the flow of the office that either the doctor or staff needed to know. The board will tell any doctor in the practice where to go next. It will tell any staff person where any doctor is presently located. It will tell the employees dealing with the schedule exactly where the practice stands as far as seeing patients on time.

Let me share an excerpt from my monthly newsletter to other efficiency-minded dentists.

> Now, how can we all harness the power of production and capacity while retaining *perfect focus* on the patient in our chair at any given time? <u>How can we see four, five, or six patients in one hour instead of just one?</u>
>
> Well, one of the ways is to utilize the **ROUTE BOARD.** Let me explain: One of the main dilemmas any dentist will face while trying to see a large volume of patients in a given day is the fear that he or she is not in the right place at the right time. Even though this has been much talked about in previous issues, I think now is a good time to address the issue again and shed some light on the subject. Maybe it will clear up some questions for the ones who are using it now. For others, I hope to get you off the fence and into the game with regards to this particular leg of the efficiency stool. I never was much of a fence sitter, but that could be because all the fences around here are either electric or barbed wire.
>
> This is certainly a tool that will give you the choice as to how much dentistry you want to provide in a given day. You will find that when you insert this one thing into your practice, you will gain minutes on every procedure you do. When you add up those minutes, you will almost certainly have the ability to work in more patients and more procedures than you can right now. You will also be doing other things that have a positive effect for your team. You will be empowering the assistants to take control of their procedures and you will also make them accountable. They will own the whole schedule and they will be forced to understand the flow of the workday. This will force

good communication with the girls up front. It will also give the schedulers the information they need up front to make good decisions about the patients they place into the workday. <u>This will almost certainly *end forever* the conflict between the hygienists and yourself.</u> The first few years of my practice were marked by the continual sight out of the corner of my eye of a hygienist leaned up against the wall at the doorway of the operatory I was working in. You know why they are there; they need you to check their patient before they can turn the room over and get the next one out of the waiting room. You know it's important for you to do that. At the same time, the clamp keeps slipping off the second molar you are working on and you are *almost finished.* So you pretend you don't see her and she pretends that she thinks you don't see her. All the while, the receptionist is getting dirty looks from the waiting room and considering whether or not she should turn in a résumé at the department store in the mall.

Best of all, *the biggest benefit is for the doctor!* It is all well and good to come up with a laundry list of things that will help your staff and your practice. I know we all feel the need to justify every decision we make. But, just for one time, <u>*can we not be just a little selfish?*</u> I totally get the fact that most dentists are such good people that we put ourselves last. Many times we will fix every little problem for the staff before we even consider helping ourselves. All the while, our backs get sore, our eyes get a little more tired, and our brains get a little more fried. Well, now you can do something to take the load off.

The Route Board is a very simple device with a very singular purpose: it allows the doctor to *focus* on the patient he or she is working on without worrying one little bit about whatever else is going on in the office. No longer do you have to wear your owner, carpenter, plumber, marketer, <u>*and*</u> doctor hats to the office. Now, you can just sit back and focus on the patient who is right in front of you. You know, the way you did when you first started out or even back in dental school. You can turn off your brain to all the chatter going on around you and build a relationship with that patient in your chair, who thought enough of you to show up for their appointment, all the while forming goodwill and gaining word-of-mouth referrals for your excellent service. When you are through with that patient, you can simply follow the route board to the next patient and focus on them.

Your staff is responsible for the board and for the route you will follow. Your staff never has to tell you anything during a procedure again. They just _tell it to the board._ All you do is happily stroll from room to room, doing exactly what the Route Board says, worrying about nothing else. You can focus on being the doctor. You will find that, over time, you also have more time to focus on the people sitting in your chairs. When your mind isn't pulling in twelve different directions, you can take a few moments to talk about their wife or kids, or whatever else important is going on in their lives. It's as close as it gets to being a trusted advisor for a busy, modern practice.

When you want to put on the owner hat at the end of the day, you will realize that you are seeing far more people with far less stress than ever before. You will also feel good about writing checks for advertising, bonuses, and expansions because you will know you now have a system that works. You will have the framework to build upon to create whatever practice type you want.

Oh, one last thing. Once you get this thing up and running, you will become so comfortable following the Route Board without a thought, that you _will follow the board wherever it says to go_. So make sure that your main assistant knows when to route you to lunch—_and don't tick her off._

From the very day we implemented that strategy into our dental practice, it changed the way we did things forever. It also catapulted us into improvements in other areas. Since then, we have implemented many other things into the practice using the Twelve Laws that have built upon the Route Board.

In what ways can you improve the logistics in your practice or business?

Every entrepreneur I know has tremendous demands on their time. They all need help in the area of scheduling or logistics. Let's look at my own daily patient schedule in my dental office. I have the variables of staff coming in on time, staff performing at proper levels of focus and efficiency, patients coming in at their appropriate scheduled time, procedure time staying on schedule, proper sequencing of appointments by the scheduler, vendors arriving on time, insurance company approval of patient benefits, patient payment issues holding up procedures, procedures changing in midstream, and many others that go on and on. Still, we manage to stay on schedule for the most part. We leave on time at night. We only see patients three days a week now, and we increased our productivity by 20 percent in our first year of practicing with these new ideas and concepts. I'll take a 20 percent increase and one more day off a week any time you want to give it to me.

Now that you have gotten into the game, gotten dirty, and learned some valuable lessons from the Law of Operations, run your ideal goal through the Law of Logistics and see what comes out the other side. This law will allow you to form some concrete, detailed directions for yourself and the other people involved in this project. Refine you schedule. When you come to a roadblock, go back in the timeline until you find the error, and then rebuild your sequence until it works. When you come out on the other side, you will have a process that you know will work.

P.P.S.

Perfectly Precise Summary

1.) Now that you have taken action, you must form a schedule.

2.) The schedule will allow you to refine the best way to implement your goal into your life.

3.) Define some tools that will allow the logistics of your goal to be made easier.

Chapter 8

Law 8: Environment
God Save the Environment!

N ow that you have successfully traversed the minefields leading up to this point and fought through them, you can rest a little easier; most of the heavy lifting on the way to implementation is done. From this point forward, you can rest your creative muscles and just follow the rest of the laws until you have conquered whatever goal you have chosen. To ensure your success, you have to create a setting around yourself that allows for maximum productivity with minimal effort. To do this, you have to standardize conditions.

There are two ways to standardize conditions. The first is to standardize yourself. This will be covered in the next chapters. The other way is to standardize the world around you to best serve your needs. In conquering our environment, we must create a standard with the outside truths so that our personality can become the pivot point on which all-else turns.

Many people only dream of attaining standardization of one thing, and even that is too much of a chore for most. If you follow the laws of this book in sequence, you will end up with a standard for both yourself and your surroundings. This will give you a powerful edge in the implementation game. In fact, most of the inhabitants of the Earth don't even attempt to standardize either themselves or the environment. Once you get this, you will be at the very top, where there is plenty of room.

Most of these laws can be intertwined to a certain extent. This one is no exception. In the previous chapter, we mentioned the need to get your records as accurate as possible. It is true that you must get them as perfect as possible to move forward in the process. It is also true that once you have standardized your environment, the measurements become more precise and the records become more accurate. Things continually get easier as you move along down this path. Then, with the better records, you will inevitably get better information that will lead to even better results.

This law will also help you master the Law of Logistics. The scheduling and intricacy of anything can only get better and more precise with the standardization of conditions. It is human nature to want to improve on achievements and set records. Of course, some are not afraid to sit idly by and keep on achieving at a certain plateau, but there will always be someone willing to put himself in peril. These will strive to beat previously unbeaten times and amass trophies yet unachieved. The foolish way to strive for those records is to try to beat the record while observing the same exact conditions as the current record holder. A smarter approach would be to try to improve as much as possible under those old conditions while planning to rethink and improve the conditions. When a breakthrough is made in the reconditioning of the environment, you won't see incremental improvements, you will see sudden record setting that races off the charts.

Think about this example from our own human history. Once, there were people who wanted to get from one place to another. The terrain was tough, and a journey between the two cities was a long, arduous one. It took so long to make the trip that few ever ventured to go there. One day, the ruler of the area thought that it would be a good thing if he created some kind of road between the two cities. He commissioned the work and it was done. When the king's highway was finished, much dirt had been moved, rocks and trees had been relocated, and a rudimentary dirt road now existed where there was none. Horses could now more easily make the journey and people could slowly walk to each city if they desired. This was a great thing, but it was still tough, especially in winter when the road became a muddy, frozen mess. At some point, someone had the idea that if they paved the road with stones, horses and people could still make the trip, even in winter. After much petitioning, the king agreed to fund this project. Some years later, the last stone was laid and a wondrous cobblestone road existed. It was a great improvement on the old dirt road, but it still had drawbacks. Sure, people could more easily walk on the road in all conditions, but it was still a long journey and it was tough to carry valuables or goods to the city because of the difficulty. Someone had seen where wheels had begun to be used in the area for different tasks. They wondered what would happen if they designed a cart and put wheels on it. Then, they could push or pull the cart and carry more things with them as they went. I imagine something like a wheelbarrow was probably used for those first trips. You know, as good as a wheelbarrow was, it wasn't long before someone put two and two together and put one of those wheeled carts behind a horse. Now you had a way to transport both people and goods from one city to the next with much less effort. This was a tremendous game changer and took travel to the next level. People created smoother and smoother roads. They created better and better wagons and carts. Eventually, they found better ways to produce horsepower than just horses. That led to motorcycles, cars, and airplanes. Now, we have space travel and who knows when we will be beaming around instantly in transport devices. The point is that it was not the slow incremental improvements that led us from the dark ages of our history. It was the change in environment that gave us real breakthroughs. Another thing to note is that as the journey in the story from one city to another got faster and faster, the trip required less effort on the part of the person making the journey.

In my dental practice, we had pretty well established the routes and methods with which we should move our supplies into the rooms. We had gotten pretty good at speed and I believe that before I started implementing color-coded templates, my staff was as efficient as anyone else in our industry. Then we tackled the problem of trying to get the supplies closer to the procedure rooms. Simultaneously, we wanted to standardize the way that the assistants gathered the supplies and presented them in preparation for a procedure on a patient. I ran this goal through the Twelve Laws, and in this excerpt from my newsletter; I'll show you what we developed. Don't let the technical jargon dissuade you from reading the passage. The broader statement is one of a solution to a goal that gave results light years ahead of previous results. This was due to a change in our environment.

> One area that has never seemingly been explored very deeply in the arena of the clinical workday is that of assistant efficiency. One thing that I have always known that was too much to ask of my assistants (even though I asked it anyway) was to set up my procedures *PERFECTLY* every time. Some of my setups require **almost one hundred little things to be just right, or more.** And I, in my great wisdom, expected my staff to perform this labor-intensive task with great speed. My own policy of "see everyone the day they want to be seen: TODAY" has led to some days where we have worked in over $12,000 worth of dentistry from new and emergency patient into an already "full" schedule. Other times, we have been overrun with nearly twenty new patients in a single day because I couldn't stand to turn anyone away. You see, there was a collision of incongruent philosophies inside my own practice that caused unnecessary tension and stress for years. In brief, I believe that if someone calls with just about any kind of need, they should be seen today. It doesn't matter to me if we are already "too full" to see them. We just tell them that we will see them today, even if they have to wait a long time or if I have to stay late. This collides headlong with the personal belief that I shouldn't just "patch" someone up. In this case, a patch for a tooth would be temporary filling and/or a prescription for the pain. Now, you can already see the train wreck coming from

a mile away. Now I assume that it is the goal of everyone here to build up a good-sized practice where the schedule stays at least relatively full. I certainly want that for myself, and have achieved it for the most part. So here we go. We are already full and the phone rings. "I'm Mr. New Patient. Please help me, I just broke a tooth!" Okay. So we say, "Sure, come on down." Somehow, we find a place to squeeze them in for an exam and X-ray. I see that they have fractured #30 down to the nerve. Remember, I am having this discussion while one patient is numbing up down the hall, and the assistant is taking a final film on a root canal in another room. "Well," I say, "Mr. Patient, you have two choices to get out of pain today: we can either take out your tooth, or we can do a root canal." Here is a good point where I am conflicted internally every day. Of course, I like doing root canals and they are worth a lot more money to the practice, but I also know that there is a waiting room full of patients who expect to be seen at the time of their appointment. You should **NEVER** forget that those folks have sacrificed at least a little of their convenience to be there on time. Also, they chose you over many others. You should never forsake these people. These are the things that go through my mind as Mr. Patient considers his options. I am secretly rooting for the extraction because I know that I can give him a block and let it soak until I can catch a little break in another appointment. Then, I can pop in, flap it, section it, and have it out in two seconds. The alternative of the endo/buildup/crown is not so fast and easy. Then the moment of truth arrives. Mr. Patient says, "You know, Doc, if I can afford it, I want to save the tooth. Can you tell me how much it will cost?" "Sure," I say. "Let me just run your insurance through the computer and we'll see what we can work out." As I trudge up the hall towards the financial coordinator, the scheduler gives me a bit of a glare. Not so obvious that I'll say something to her, but it is there nonetheless; she knows that if Mr. Patient gets his root canal today, her schedule will be shot—and just wait until the assistants get hold of the information that I want them to work in *another* big procedure.

The scenario I just described played out just about like that for a long time. I couldn't turn people away, and I consistently put my staff in unworkable situations. I was the one with the deep beliefs that led to the problem in the first place, so I didn't mind killing myself, but I knew that I couldn't do that to my staff over and over without losing some of them, probably the best ones. I had to either find a way to feel good about telling people that I just couldn't see them today or find a way to get the job done so fast and effectively that I wasn't killing my staff.

I just couldn't do it. I couldn't tell people that even though they had chosen to call my office when they could have called a hundred more (well, not really—I live out in the sticks, so they could have called maybe five more in town) dentists, that they would have to wait a week, a month, whatever. I decided that there had to be a way to solve the bottlenecks in my practice that were stopping us from being able to deliver the care in a timely and efficient manner. First, I took lots and lots of CE. I wanted to make sure that the problem wasn't me or the way I was delivering the actual dentistry. It helped some as we eliminated wasted motions and got more modern equipment, but not enough. Lots of times, I would get caught up myself and have to wait for another room to open up. One of the next things I tried was to expand the office from three to seven operatories. This really helped. Now at least we had somewhere to sit people down in a dental chair instead of the waiting room. As things got better again, I learned a hard lesson: *It doesn't matter how many rooms you have if you don't have enough staff members to man all the rooms.* I could get caught up myself, but every single assistant would be finishing up a procedure, checking out a patient, or cleaning and resetting a room. That would leave me either waiting around again or starting procedures without any help, one of my least favorite things in the world to do.

Finally, we hit pay dirt. We came up with a system for the assistants to use when turning over a room that cut that time down more than in half. And the added side effect that we weren't expecting was that the room setups were now *perfect every time*. Even though this had always been my goal, it had never worked out. My assistants always had to leave the room to get some little something that they had forgotten to set up. I had tried to solve this with checklists to little avail a couple of years earlier. They had told me that the checklists were just too long and that we had too many of them to try to sort through and check off every item while patients were waiting to be seated. I had tried again to levy a penalty system against them if I had to ask for something and it wasn't right there where it was supposed to be. This eventually flopped too. It seems that the back staff felt they were being penalized while the front staff was not. This was a good argument, because I had no good way of policing the front, even though they invariably made mistakes. It was just that the mistakes on the clinical side usually happened right in front of me.

I believe that most of the problems I had in getting consistent and perfect setups from my staff had occurred when I placed stress on the system, like when I worked in extra root canals and such. I mean, if I had given the assistant two hours to prepare for the next appointment, I'm sure everything would have been perfect every time—but I didn't. I expected it to take just a few short minutes. With much trial and error, what we developed was a system of color-coded templates for the operatories and matching color-coding for the central stocking area. This allows the assistants to match up all the items for their procedures visually. This dramatically decreases the amount of time needed to get the rooms ready. We also stole an idea from the restaurant industry; we took most of our sterilization and disposal from chair side to one common area, reducing the number of steps required to be taken by the staff by over half again. What few things we have left that aren't covered by the templates and the color coding, we have boiled down to a checklist algorithm that gets 95 percent of the offices procedure checklists onto ONE sheet of paper. No longer do we have to hunt everywhere for the right checklist. It's always right there.

I guess the main thing that this new system has offered me is the ability to keep my core beliefs intact. Now, instead of moans and groans from my staff when I say, "We'll be working in a root canal, core, and crown on tooth #19." I hear three beautiful words: "No problem, Doc."

This template system has to be the most brilliant thing that I ever came up with on my own. This takes most of the real thinking out of the setup of each procedure room. Another area where we greatly improved our environment was by developing a color-coded room that now houses the supplies for each procedure. That room has rows of bins that are colored to match the templates for each procedure. All my assistants have to do is go into that color-coded room, put color-coded supplies from each colored row into a basket, and take the supplies into the procedure room. There, they pull a color-coded template off the wall and place the color-coded supplies on the corresponding color of the template. When all the colored blocks are full, we are ready to treat the patient.

An unexpected benefit of all this was that when we took the burden of remembering the hundreds of variables of each procedure off the shoulders of the assistants, our business greatly increased. One of the statistical areas that improved was in patient referrals. This is the area that describes when a current patient recommends another person to our practice. This is the greatest compliment we can have. One of the things that our patients say they like about our office is that our staff always has time to talk to them. I assume that the only factor that could have changed to improve this stat is that the assistants don't have to think so much about their room setups. Now, they can chit-chat and make small talk while they set up the room. They also just have more overall time to spend building a relationship with the patient because I have shortened their cycle time. It has certainly been a win-win for everyone.

P.P.S.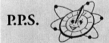

Perfectly Precise Summary

1.) You must put yourself in the best situation to continue your success.

2.) The surroundings are of vital importance.

3.) Even if a goal is attained, you will revert back to your old ways without making the goal easier to retain.

Chapter 9

=====

Law 9: Standard Operating Procedures
Keeping the Dark Ages at Bay

Now that you have gotten through all the super-duper fun stuff, it is time to hit you with some heavy lifting. No, this part will not be fun, but it must be done to solidify the work you have done up until now. You must set the standard you have created and place it into permanent residence in your life or business. The best way to do this is with a standard operating procedure, or SOP for short.

Why has the human race, with all its intellect and ingenuity, failed to accomplish more in its time on Earth? We can all look inward and see how much we have personally accomplished in our time on this planet. If you consider all the thousands and millions of great minds that preceded us, one would think that great and glorious wonders would exist all around. Perpetual problems and strife should have been long gone. Disease and war should be a distant memory, right? Why has this progress been so exceedingly slow? There have been great thinkers and leaders from way back to ancient Greece up until the modern day. There have been plans, schedules, logistics, and operations for ages. So little innovation has endured to be built upon. Ingenuity has ebbed and flowed. Children have continued to make the mistakes of their fathers. Those great thinkers came and went and took their great ideas with them. Sure, we have made progress, but not as much as we should have made. We know that Archimedes invented amazing war machines for the defense of Syracuse against the Romans, but we don't have the plans. We know that the Coliseum in Rome is still standing. Does anyone think we could build a concrete structure of that size today that would be standing several thousand years later? Doubtful. Where is the recipe for their stone mixture they used?

Each one of the preceding laws of time up to this point can and should be tested and reduced to written, permanent standard operating instructions so that you and those around you may understand the entire goal and the reasons behind it. This is at the heart of this law. Who else will write this new standard? The time and research required to bring an outsider in to do it for you would take considerable effort and funds. Outside people will have their own ideas and takes on things. You certainly don't want to derail the train of thought that has survived the tests in this book so far. You are the president, CEO, and chairman of the board of this particular goal. Take hold of the reins and grab your rightful responsibility. Write your own standard and be glad. You are almost there. Your goal is within sight.

What are SOPs?

Any official, written document that sets forth an operational guideline is defined as a standard operating procedure. SOPs are not training materials; they build on training, providing an organizational blueprint for operational safety and efficiency. Too much or too little detail in SOPs limits their usefulness and effectiveness. You know all the problems that companies, small businesses, mom-and-pop businesses, and regular people face with keeping their systems rolling along intact, right? Well, these problems may have been avoided if the new organization had implemented written guidelines that defined precisely how operations were to be conducted. These guidelines, called standard operating procedures, clearly spell out what is expected and required of personnel during any and every business-related procedure. They provide a mechanism to communicate requirements, organizational policies, and strategic plans to all the employees of a company or group. A common definition of a standard operating procedure is "an organized list of directives that establish a standardized course of action." In other words, SOPs are written guidelines that explain what is expected and required of anyone performing their jobs. A comprehensive set of SOPs defines in significant detail how the organization plans to operate. In short, they get everybody on the same page. SOPs are not intended to duplicate technical information or provide step-by-step instructions for doing the job; these are called policies. SOPs provide the framework within which these more detailed policies exist. The knowledge and skills that individuals need to perform specific job tasks are addressed in more detailed descriptions. Standard operating procedures instead describe related information such as the use of supplies, equipment maintenance, duties of personnel, command structures, coordination with other organizations, reporting requirements, and so forth.

Stated differently, SOPs don't describe how to do the job in a precise technical fashion, they describe the department's rules for doing the job and give procedural guidance. An example might help to clarify this point. Operating a piece of equipment requires both technical skills and procedural guidance. Well-designed SOPs help fill both needs. For individual workers, SOPs clarify job requirements and expectations in a format that can be readily applied on the job. They explain in detail what the department wants them to do in the situations they are most likely to encounter. The result is improved safety, performance, and morale. For department managers, the advantages are equally great. SOPs provide a mechanism to identify needed changes, articulate strategies, document intentions, implement regulatory requirements, enhance training, and evaluate operational performance. The result is improved operational efficiency, greater accountability, and reduced liability. Once they are created, the entire operation benefits.

How do we make our SOP?

In this example I will assume a group setting. At the beginning of the process, members must clearly define the mission, goals, and objectives, including a projected timeframe for completing the goal. Guidance from management should address such factors as the authority of the group, budget, and available resources, and the desired end product. The team leader should then clarify expectations of individual members, including work assignments and standards of conduct in the development process. Meeting minutes and agendas should be prepared and distributed to members on a regular basis if meetings are held. Members should also document the work of the team to ensure accountability and to provide a written record of group proceedings for future reference.

Write the SOP

Just like everything else we've talked about, you've got to get up and actually do this. After a procedure has been selected, the next task faced is the actual creation of a written document. To be effective and usable by you or your personnel, SOPs must be written clearly and concisely, using a logical and consistent format. The following suggestions for writing SOPs will enhance the user-friendliness of the final product, a key variable in determining success or failure during implementation.

What level of detail should the SOP have?

Generally speaking, SOPs should provide only broad procedural guidelines, not specific details of task performance. For example, a new SOP may include guidance to *"Make our customers feel comfortable by using good phone etiquette."* However, too much detail is provided if the SOP describes related job tasks, such as, *"(1) Always answer the phone using your name and thanking them for calling; (2) Have your book of common objections open and waiting when the customer calls; (3) Never ask them yes-or-no questions; and (4) Always ask for their name during the beginning of the phone call."* Remember: SOPs are not training manuals; they are broad organizational guidelines for performing tasks that members have already been trained to accomplish safely and effectively. Policies can and should be written after the SOPs have been established.

SOP Topic Areas

The most common areas and the ones I use are:

1.) Purpose: This is why you are doing this in the first place.
2.) Scope: This should make clear which areas are affected by this SOP and which are not.
3.) Definitions: Clearly defines the terms that will be used to describe the SOP.
4.) Description: This should describe all the factors involved in this project. This will be one of the bulkier areas of the SOP.
5.) Training: This tells everyone what training is required to master the new goal.
6.) Personnel Involved: A list of the people who will be part of this SOP.
7.) Procedure: A step-by-step walk through the expected standard.
8.) Equipment: Any outside equipment that might be needed.
9.) Precautions: A list of potential pitfalls associated with this new standard.
10.) Reference: This is a list of references that one might need for clarification about this SOP.

SOPs are statements that summarize behavioral requirements and expectations in a certain functional area (e.g., expected behavior in worker areas, training and education, adherence to policies and protocols among many others). Typically, SOPs also contain some narrative material that explains, for example, the purpose and intent of the guidelines and possible exceptions. The subjects addressed and level of detail in SOPs may vary from department to department. In general, however, SOP writers try to provide enough guidance to control operations without overwhelming personnel or unnecessarily limiting flexibility in special situations.

Writing SOPs

SOPs should be organized into a logical framework, using headings and sub-headings that help clarify functional relationships and the roles played by different groups. Most experts recommend that departments divide the SOP manual into separate sections for administration and operations. In our dental office, that would be *clinical* and *clerical*. A mail-order business might be *operations* and *fulfillment*. If desired, operational SOPs can be further subdivided into units that separately address each major component of the organization's mission. Personnel policies may be covered in a separate document or set of documents.

Always use clarity and conciseness. SOPs should be clear, concise, and written in plain English. While simply regurgitating proprietary language is easy for the owner of the business or the developer of the SOP, such language is often difficult to understand and apply to operational situations. Clear and simple statements are the best way to describe actions in SOPs. Using an outline or bulleted style instead of a continuous narrative simplifies the presentation of information and helps clarify relationships among different components of the SOP.

What target audience should you shoot for? Write for the majority of the group or company. Some members may require more help understanding the SOP than others. Others might already be highly experienced in the subject area. Generally, SOPs should be written to address the needs and educational level of the majority of department members, using language they can easily understand. Of course, also write these so that you can go back and recommit yourself if you let them slip. We will discuss that more in an upcoming chapter.

What about flexibility and ambiguity? To be effective, organizational guidelines must be unambiguous. At the same time, SOPs should provide enough flexibility for the on-scene leader to make decisions based on the situation at hand. Balancing the need to reduce ambiguity while maintaining flexibility can be difficult. Department SOPs should be precise but inherently flexible, permitting an acceptable level of discretion that reflects the nature of the situation and the judgment of the team leader. (This concept should be explicitly stated at the beginning of the office SOP manual if this is an SOP for a business.) A related issue involves use of the terms *shall* and *may* when writing SOPs. An action preceded by the word "shall" is generally considered to be an inviolate rule, while using the term *may* implies greater flexibility and discretion by personnel. However, simply using *may* as an antecedent for every action can reduce the effectiveness of SOPs and lead to unnecessary ambiguity. By the same token, certain actions are so critical to health and safety that the term *shall* is obligatory (e.g., *"personnel shall not reach down and touch any surgical instrument that has fallen to the floor during the procedure."* SOPs must be written clearly, concisely, and unambiguously. They should be organized and presented in a manner that is user-friendly and readily accessible during operations. All department personnel should understand that, with the exception of critical health and safety issues (identified by the term *shall*), SOPs can be modified to suit the rarities of a particular situation, based on the judgment of the team member or team leader. A clear understanding by all department personnel of the purpose and function of SOPs will help eliminate confusion and misunderstanding. A standardized format or layout for SOPs helps streamline the writing process. Additional benefits include improved integration of new SOPs into the department's larger SOP manual, ease of revision or updating, and enhanced usability. Different formats may be used for

SOPs depending on the intended audience and purpose. For example, SOPs intended for clinical operations may be formatted differently than operational protocols used by office personnel. Regardless of their intended use, however, several items are usually included in any SOP other than the ones we discussed above are:

- Numbering system—Important for reference, usability, and integrating individual SOPs into the overall manual.
- Effective date—Date the SOP is officially adopted for use in the field. (This may be different from the date of issue. The effective date may be purposefully later than the date of issue to allow for all department members to be informed and/or educated on the new SOP.)
- Expiration/review date—Important for ensuring the currency of SOPs by establishing a date for periodic review and revision, if needed.
- Title—For ease of reference and usability.
- Authority signature(s)—Indicates that the SOP was properly created, reviewed, and approved by the leader, boss, or head authority.

An organized, methodical development process is the best approach for preparing effective and valid SOPs. The process should be conceived as an integrated whole, and as such, its success is determined by the sum of its parts. The quality of SOPs will largely reflect the composition and leadership of the company or group itself, the level of support provided by the team, the team's ability to establish realistic goals and acceptable procedures, the nature of research and analysis performed by the team, and the team's ability to select appropriate alternatives and justify the results.

While certain elements are usually incorporated in all SOPs, a variety of different formats is possible, depending on the purpose and intended audience. Review and testing are vitally important for ensuring that potential problems or conflicts are identified prior to finalizing SOPs. The boss, leader, CEO, or head jerk in charge is ultimately responsible.

SOPs have many other applications and benefits for any individual or organization, including:

- Explanation of expectations—SOPs describe and document what is expected of personnel in the performance of their official duties. As such, they provide a benchmark for personnel, an objective mechanism for evaluating operational performance, and a tool for promoting a positive fellowship. **Everyone knows their own job description.**

- Standardization of roles and job descriptions—SOPs identify planned and agreed-upon roles and actions. This information helps standardize activities and promote coordination and communications among personnel. SOPs also simplify decision-making requirements under potentially stressful conditions. **People know what to do when the going gets tough.**

- Training systems—Written SOPs can provide the framework for training programs, member briefings, drills, and exercises. These activities, in turn, improve the understanding of work requirements and help identify potential problems. A comprehensive SOP manual also serves as a self-study and reference document for personnel. **Stay on top with proven systems.**

- Feedback about current systems—The process of researching and developing SOPs provides opportunities for managers or leaders to compare current work practices with the state of the art in their field. Feedback from outside groups, technical experts, and staff can help to identify potential problems and solutions. **Know why it needs to be done this way.**

- Communications to others—SOPs clarify the department's operational philosophy and recommended practices. As such, they may prove useful in communicating intentions and requirements to outside groups, or enhancing other's understanding of the business or activity. **Show others how to do it.**

Now that I have bored you to death, let me try to break down why you should care about these things. First off, if you are reading this book, I know that you are an achiever. Achievers generally cannot achieve one thing and be done with it forever. They have to continually take the next hill. The SOP lets you spend a lot of time getting one single aspect of something perfect. Then, once you have mustered the courage to fight off procrastination and actually set this thing down in writing, you can set it aside, delegate it to someone else, and move on to the next big thing in your life or business. This will allow you to have creative freedom and pick your next battle, and, yet you know that things are taken care of on the home front. This SOP and the ensuing SOP manual that will inevitably exist after a few of these things get written will give your business the systematization that you need. If you want to step away from things for a week, month, or year, you will know that if your SOPs are being followed, your business will still be in tip-top shape when you get back. Also, some entrepreneurs I know are bad about getting to the top and then getting lazy. They will slide back down to pre-SOP levels after a while and may not even remember the steps that got them to the top. All they have to do is dust off the old SOP manual, open it up, and voila! Instant success is back at their fingertips.

Now that you're convinced that these things are essential (they are a law, for goodness sake), let's get down and dirty and write up one for the goal you are currently working on.

P.P.S.

Perfectly Precise Summary

1.) A SOP is a necessity to remember how a goal was achieved and why.

2.) Follow the above steps to write your own for each goal.

3.) Make a SOP manual to house all your goal SOPs and the reference material that goes with each.

Chapter 10

Law 10: Discipline
Keep It Together

There can be organization without discipline—for a season. It can exist, but not for long. Even in a situation where discipline has been installed, if that discipline is weakened for a moment, the progress of centuries can be lost. The integrity of all things depends on the discipline that keeps the process intact.

Could anyone doubt the discipline exhibited by the famous fighters of Sparta? I'm sure you know the story: King Leonidas of Sparta led 300 of his best men against the Persian ruler Xerxes. The Persians numbered in the hundreds of thousands. The Spartans were so well trained and disciplined that they held off the insurmountable force for seven days to try to block the Persians' entrance into Greece. This resulted in one of the most famous battles in history. The valor and discipline of the Spartans became legend and led to future victories by the Greeks, who used the memory of the fallen heroes as a rallying cry. This is an extreme example, but proof positive that amazing feats can be achieved if these laws are followed.

A disciplined life is the result of a steady growth and years of patiently doing the right thing. Look at the master sculptor: the master doesn't strike a likeness all in one blow and say, "Good enough." It may very well be that a casual observer might find that first rough out appealing and more beautiful than many sculptures around. No, the final product is painfully and laboriously wrought. It is a slow work over a period of time, and when the master is through, the likeness comes alive in a way that can be copied by no other. In the same way, we have to fashion our goal into perfection each day. We cannot simply succeed one time and set it aside in the corner to decay and weaken. Unlike the sculptor, we are never truly through with our goal. We must gaze but a moment at our final result and then press equally hard to maintain it. Our goals are not made from marble or granite. They are subject to flitter away the second we let down our guard.

Modern-day sports are another place to look to see the power of discipline. If you will notice, it is rare that you see the same team winning a championship two years in a row. When it does happen, it is cause for study and reflection. Those teams who managed to put together continuous championships all had several qualities that allowed this. Remember that in professional sports in America, the teams are very closely matched in skill level from the top to the bottom of the league. It is peculiar that there are commonly perennial winners and perennial losers due to this fact. However, it is a fact. This must mean that success at that level depends heavily on intangible factors, like the ones we have been learning about in this book. On those teams with the consecutive championships, you will find high individual standards, extreme accountability to the other players, extreme discipline, and severe penalties for team infractions. For a team to win frequently in professional sports, discipline must be at the core of every action they take. They certainly don't take for granted the fact that just because they are champions today, they will be forever. They know that they must work at it every day.

There is a story of a dinner party of several accomplished men in a large metropolitan city. The story goes that over dessert, the conversation turned to the innate qualities of self-made and successful men. In turn, each man admitted that they belonged to that class—with one exception. When it came time for a certain bishop to acknowledge this simple truth to the club, he remained silent. He looked like he was pondering the proper thing to say. The host, a very industrious young businessman, was always on the lookout for wisdom. He wished to draw out the bishop and hear his thoughts. Most of the men at the table had already assumed that the bishop would say that he was not self-made, but was a success by the will of God. This would have been an acceptable answer and one not completely unexpected for a man in his vocation. What he said spoke volumes and was not what any of them had expected to hear, except perhaps the young host. Upon the request for his thoughts, the bishop simply said, "I am not made yet." You could write whole volumes of books on the truths those five words contained. So long as life exists, for better or worse, we will be challenged with tests both good and evil. Until the moment we die, our character will be shaped by forces both outside and inside. Discipline is our only chance to keep hold of any accomplishment, and even then, our success is not guaranteed. However, discipline will give us our best and only chance to maintain a goal once it has been reached.

> *"Disregarding the honors that most men value, and looking to the truth, I shall endeavor in reality to live as virtuously as I can, and when I die to die so. And I invite all other men to the utmost of my power; and you too I in turn invite to this contest, which I affirm surpasses all contests here."* – **Plato**

Let's consider an extreme case of discipline before we break down this law into something useful.

There was a certain man from England in the 1500s who came to believe in God, even though there was no English translation of the Bible at the time. His name was William Tyndale and he later came to be associated with the religious movement known as the Reformers. The Church in Rome held all power over Christendom at the time, and Tyndale became a strong believer that the Bible should be translated into a language that even the common people could understand. Tyndale was an educated man and was soon accepted into the clergy of the day. He loved the common man and made it his ideal goal to translate the scriptures so they could understand and better commune with God. He set out on his work. He painstakingly translated several books of the Old Testament and got them into print. This became a point of severe contention between Tyndale and the clergy hierarchy in England. Tyndale believed that they wanted to keep the people confused and superstitious more than they wanted to help them. He began to make enemies of priests around the country. Finally, he was forced to flee England and continue his work elsewhere. He even overcame a tremendous setback to his mission; his ship was lost in one of his journeys, and all his work, notes, writings, and research were lost with it. He forced himself to move forward and recreate his work all over again. His translations were able to take advantage of new printing innovations, so they soon became sought after. Tyndale became famous even though he was now located in Belgium. A high-ranking cardinal from England had finally had enough; he sent word that Tyndale was to be arrested and brought to justice for crimes against the Church. He even had the emperor's decree. Tyndale was captured and charged. He was offered a lawyer but refused. While imprisoned, he managed to convert his keeper, his keeper's daughter, and others of their household. Finally, when Tyndale's enemies had failed utterly to force him to renounce his "heretic" ways, he was found guilty and sentenced to be burned at the stake. His last words as he was tied to the stake were, "Lord! Open the King of England's eyes."[7] So he passed from this world without damaging his ideal goal in life. His work lived on; much of his translation passed into the King James Version, the most widely read version of the Bible. How many of us would have had the discipline to continue in the face of hardship, persecution, and certain death like this phenomenal man? I would have probably quit when the boat sank. I have almost lost my mind the few times that my computer lost a couple of thousand words before I could save them. Remember that Tyndale lived in a world without search engines and backups. The other stuff is just unimaginable. I'll try hard not to get into anything that heavy again, but it makes the point.

Some men are born with strong wills. Others are reasonable or weak, but can be trained. It is not a weak-minded individual who can stand up to all the forces and distractions of life to stand strong. The Law of

---

7   *Fox's Book of Martyrs.* Forbush, William B. The John Winston Company. Philadelphia, PA, 1926.

Discipline regularly tosses people around with ruthlessness. Anyone who doesn't recognize the strength required to consistently keep their achievements secure is doomed to lose those achievements over time. True success hinges upon this fact, but it is hard to find someone willing to put good conscious effort into its maintenance.

Perfect discipline exists in nature, too. It is actually everywhere in nature, but especially in the worlds of animals or insects that live in groups, colonies, or hives. Think about a beehive: no bee appears to obey any other bee, yet the workings of the hive are so precise that every bee is engrossed in his or her special little task. This discipline is driven by instinct and pushes the bees to work together for the common good. If a drone fails to become useful, the working bees become aware and do away with them. It's a pretty harsh punishment, but the hive lives on. In the ant kingdom, leafcutter ants do amazing things. There are several different types of these ants with their own jobs. They even have a system to cut leaves into smaller and smaller pieces, each size cut to a different specification by a different type of ant. This goes on until a very specialized ant feeds the leaves to a special fungus that lives deep inside the colony. All the ants then live off the nutrients of the fungus. This is a tremendous system that requires complete discipline to continue the life of the process.

Let's go over some of the dangers out there waiting to ensnare you and take away your discipline.

- **Love of action:** The entrepreneur is especially susceptible to this one. These people usually love climbing mountains. They love the journey. Even when riches are involved, these people find wealth a secondary motive. They love the hunt and they love the chase. These people exist on impulse. This is a great quality to own when you are driving through the laws in this book on the way to your ideal goal. This quality becomes a burden once the goal has been attained and success is visible. Then, the spirit grows restless and wants for greener pastures and new frontiers. Oftentimes, the old achieved goal—however monumental and wondrous—gets left discarded on the side of the adventurer's path. The strength of the person becomes the weakness in the end. To exercise discipline, this person will have to constantly keep their mind focused on remembering this achieved goal and why it was important. Then, they will have a chance to keep it in pristine condition.

- **Indecision:** Some people have much difficulty attaining a clear view of any situation. They have trouble seeing the essential elements of a situation. They can't easily weigh motives, consider the future, or avoid unintended consequences. They may have been able to push through the laws to achieve their goal, but once that goal is secured, the old habits creep back in. These people drift along, and when trouble or temptation comes along, they will find it difficult to form a good plan of defense. The best way for this person to sustain his or her discipline is to keep a constant watch for things that might hurt or destroy that achievement. Know that sometimes people will come upon a situation where they must make a decision or lose all they have worked for. Think about the things that might do that to your goal before they happen, and consider what your recourse would be. Be ready for the problem before it actually happens.

- **Waste of thought:** This has gotten far worse in recent history. Now, it is completely possible for a gifted thinker to allow himself to sink into a comfortable place and just be entertained. The age of information has not made us all smarter. Sure, some of the accomplishments could not exist without these technologies, but for the most part, they have become a prison or trap. Good, strong-minded people and weak-minded people alike have fallen into the traps set by Internet sites, social networking sites, and abundant television and music choices. It seems that we have created a fur-lined cage for ourselves. Sure, it is comfortable. It is enjoyable for a season, but there will eventually be a reckoning when people realize how much time they wasted being entertained. Don't forget that time is the only currency in the world that you can never accumulate more than your allotted portion. Don't get sucked in.

• **Weak action:** This is one of the most common problems plaguing the world today. It seems everywhere that people just can't get up off the rear ends and do anything worthwhile. Their innumerable failures of life are due primarily to a lack of will power. They may have found the inner strength to get up and accomplish one goal, but as soon as that one was finished, they flopped right back onto the couch. You hear stories about lazy people who had a life-changing experience and became superstars in their field, working tirelessly day and night for the common good. I'll bet there are 999 stories for each one of those about people who thought it would be a good idea to accomplish something, but never did one thing about it. If you are that person, and you have this inclination and you still managed to get this far in the book, there is hope. Just know that you will have to manage the Law of Discipline harder than most if you want to maintain your achievement.

> *"There was probably never a man endowed with such remarkable gifts who accomplished so little that was worthy of them…"*—**Thomas de Quincy**, speaking of a gifted nineteenth-century classical composer

How can we guard against these weaknesses that would rob us of our gains?

Believe in yourself at all times. Never lose that deep-down belief that you gained your goal through good, hard work of your own doing. Believe that nothing can take this achievement away from you, but fight like heck if something tries. You may be spattered with blood from the fights you encounter along the way. Let not your heart be troubled; those red specks signify your willingness to defend your prize.

Perseverance

I think one trait that cannot be separated from discipline is stick-to-itiveness or perseverance. To overcome your own list of personal dangers in committing to discipline and going forward, you must bring your entire attention to the matter involved. You must thoroughly think of the motives involved in the situation. You must think of the potential outcomes of remaining true or falling away from your original intent. Then, we must resolve to do anything and everything necessary to turn our mind away from our weakness and toward the preservation of our goal. We say that we want to do this, yet much of the time, we don't really resolve to do it. This is not optional if you want to succeed; this is necessity. If you can resolve to persevere, that is surely a harbinger of success later on.

Sometimes you have to know your own self so well that you just have to cut off any temptation of weakness to succeed. If you have achieved the goal of losing weight and you have a severe weakness for dessert, you might want to physically throw away all the junk food in the house and buy no more. Some people would say that you lack will power if you did such a thing. I say you just know yourself well enough to not put yourself in a bad position. You are setting yourself up for success.

Mark Twain once declared to his physician, who had accused him of binging too much on tobacco, coffee, tea, bad foods, and hot scotches, "I can't make a reduction in these things because I lack the will power. I can cut them off entirely, but I can't merely modify them." Of course, this is funny because just about everything Mark Twain uttered was funny. And like many of his statements, it held a deeper truth than the superficial obvious. He showed remarkable good sense by that statement. He knew that if he were to deprive himself of some of his favorite indulgences, he would have to remove them entirely from his life. The Bible even says, *"Wherefore if they hand or thy foot offend thee, cut them off, and cast them from thee: it is better for thee to enter into life halt or maimed, rather than having two hands or two feet to be cast into everlasting fire. And if thine eye offend thee, pluck it out, and cast it from thee: it is better for thee to enter into life with one eye, rather than having two eyes to be cast into hell fire"* –Matthew 18:8.

That statement is in the Bible more than once. Hopefully we have interpreted the advice as figurative and not literal, but the reasoning behind it is simple and true. It does little good to have to find the strength to overcome desire over and over again. Every time you say no, it chips away a little bit at your resolve. The desire will continue to assert itself. Somehow, at some time in the future, you will eventually give in to your weakness. You have to find the power to turn away the desire toward weakness the moment it enters your mind. Once you can do this, you will have begun to master your own will. You know have the tools you need to persevere and follow the Law of Discipline.

Focus

The last part that I want to make sure not to overlook in this chapter is *focus*. Focus can make average people look like supermen, and it can make mental giants look like shiftless bums. Don't ever fail to give the proper amount of attention to any worthwhile project. When you are attempting to work through this book with a goal, or in any situation in life where focus is needed, do whatever you need to do to get your mind right. When I began to see many more dental patients in my practice than I ever had, I feared that my focus might slip. I certainly didn't want that to happen. I wanted to give each patient the attention they deserved. I also wanted to make sure that quality of work wasn't sacrificed to speed. That is when I implemented a system in my office called the route board. It allowed me to free my mind from all the whirlwind of hectic things going on in my office and focus on one patient at a time.

Don't worry about loss of production time when you focus on something the way you should. You will more than make up for the time investment later on when things go much more smoothly than they would have otherwise. Ask yourself this: "Is it better that I tweet, update my social media, and e-mail six things in the next ten minutes—or that I sit in a quiet place and really get my thoughts in order on this one important goal?" I think we all know the answer.

P.P.S.

Perfectly Precise Summary
1.) Without discipline, all goals will eventually be lost.
2.) You must place into your mind that you will retain the goal achievement at all cost.
3.) Define your greatest weaknesses and form a detailed plan to deal with each one.
4.) Use your powers of perseverance and focus to fight off these weaknesses.

Chapter 11

Law 11: Motivation
If you can't get excited about this …

It's time to dive back into the rah-rah world. Our trip through the implementation of a goal has shifted squarely back into the realm of thought. Motivation may be an invisible force, but it is very powerful. Motivation has been a driving power throughout all times. It is doubtful that any of the wonders of the ancient or modern world would have ever existed without some form of motivation. Motivation doesn't only reside in the latter portion of the laws; it cascades over most all of the other laws in some form or fashion. Its residence as the eleventh law is not an accident, though. Motivation comes easily as one enters the linear pursuit through these laws. Immediately after the a-ha moment, the blood is racing, the adrenaline is flowing, and expectations are at an all-time high. Enthusiasm, a close relative in the motivation family, is so present that it seems improbable that the river of energy you are experiencing associated with the pursuit of this goal will ever run dry. At this point in your journey, you wonder why you haven't already done something like this and you question the will power of all others who should have already accomplished something like this.

Let me share an experience with you that may explain what I am talking about. A few years ago, I attended a conference in Boston with my best friend. As part of the experience, dentists attending could participate in a bicycle ride on the Freedom Trail, a stretch of road that ran through Boston for several miles. It was supposedly the exact path that Paul Revere rode while shouting, "The British are coming!" We agreed to sign up and set our pre-goal as the successful completion of this bike trip. Both my friend and I were okay bike riders; we were experts by no means. By *okay*, I mean that we could ride bicycles in the large, open spaces of the South to which we were accustomed, without falling over very often. We thought we had taken our first bike trail ride seriously. I even bought a new bike and rode for an hour or so each night for a month leading up to our trip. The day of the ride, we met the other riders in the lobby. After we exchanged pleasantries with the other obviously more experienced bikers, we boarded a bus that took us to a spacious park where we would begin our long ride. Both my friend and I were psyched. It didn't look so hard in this big, green park on this beautiful spring day. We had motivation galore at this point. We were in a jocular mood and poked fun with each other. The itinerary was that we would ride several miles to another park, eat lunch, and ride back. As we took off, we were riding side by side and I commented that these bikes were a little more complicated than the one I had been riding back home. My friend agreed, but this didn't seem to pose much of a problem at this point. The first mile or so of the ride was in a big park on a path that seemed about the size of a small-town airport runway. Then I noticed something funny on the gray path ahead. There was a stripe down the center of the path and the concrete width narrowed considerably. The path became so narrow that my friend and I had to go single file now, instead of side by side. We were a little more unsure about our surroundings and we dropped toward the back of the pack of riders. Still, we were doing fine. Suddenly, the path broke free from the tree-lined park and became little more than a sidewalk on the side of an eight-lane highway. Whoa, this just got interesting. At about the same time, I learned what that single stripe down the center of the path was for. I learned this as the handlebars of a biker going in the opposite direction brushed against my handlebars. This thing had just gotten real. I tensed up completely. I did not expect that I would have to hold my bike inside one half of a path that was barely the width of a sidewalk. The chitchat subsided as both my friend and I had to increase our concentration to avoid an embarrassing and potentially harmful wreck with another biker. Our motivation was definitely waning. Things only got worse as the Charles River now appeared on my right side. Are you kidding me? I now have accomplished riders zipping past on my left, occasionally swiping paint with my bike, and a plunge to certain death on my right if I can't stay on the two-foot-wide piece of concrete on which I am plodding along. I also have the stress of trying to keep pace with the group. All of the pack seemed to be effortlessly flying down this Freedom Trail as if they had all been Boston natives and training for this day their entire lives. Somehow, we made it to the lunchtime park. We wheeled in and parked our bikes. As we ate lunch, my friend and I shared a look that we both completely understood. We couldn't bear the idea of getting back on our bikes for the ride home. At this point, our motivation for finishing the complete Freedom Trail on bike was at an all-time low. If this had been an important goal, we could have pushed through our doubts with the use of motivation and ridden back. As it stood, we just didn't want to ride back. We had underestimated the ride and we decided to shift our goal. Now, we just wanted to get back to our hotel before dark. This was certainly a goal we could get behind. We asked the tour guide if we could quit. He called his supervisor and got permission for us to lock up our bikes at this park until someone could come back for them. We asked the guide where the Hyatt was and he pointed to a small, dark spot in the in the distant cityscape. He said it was about four miles away. The unfortunate thing was that we hadn't brought our wallets on the bike ride and had no money or plastic on us. We decided to walk back. Motivation wasn't very hard to come by for this particular goal because we were a couple of foreigners in a strange land trying to get safely home. You can see where motivation played a key role in several decisions of that day.

It is not simply enough to say that motivation is important. To truly master this law, you need to go deeper into the psyche. You have to define your core self and you have figure out what motivates you specifically. First, you have to get past all the things that you think really motivate you. You can say that money motivates you, but if that is true, you would be in the great minority. You could say that power motivates you, but, once again, you would be in the minority. True motivations are deeper inside and probably could be completely explained ad nauseam by psychologists and psychiatrists. I will try to give the abbreviated country boy version of true motivations.

There are only a few big categories of true motives, in my opinion.

<u>Social motivation:</u> People who are motivated by this are usually more interested in the cementation and propagation of social connections and affiliations than anything else. They may enjoy stature if it improves their standing in their own community. They will not try to achieve anything drastic if it means they will be isolated and cut off from their current affinity group. It is also hard for these people to be bosses or managers, because they always care about what others think of them. Other people's opinions are big motivators for them.

<u>Achievement motivation:</u> These types are not above making money or gaining power, but it is not the primary motivator in their lives. They will often seek out big challenges. If they are the first to attempt something or if the reward is very great, they will be first in line. They certainly don't mind being aloof and separated from the herd if that seems to be the best way to succeed toward their goal. If this type of person is placed in a job that doesn't give incentive, opportunities for advancement, or clear feedback in the pursuit of goals, they will probably just sit there in the middle of the pack. To the untrained

eye, the achievement-motivated person in such a job will look average. However, once an incentive is added or there is a chance to progress in a very difficult challenge, watch out. These people will then leave their peers behind in the dust. If you can keep the achievement potential fresh and new, these types will go in high gear forever. Just don't let them get bored or complacent. They are not so much out for recognition as for the thrill of the game. Recognition usually goes hand in hand with these types, but it is not their primary focus.

Outcome motivation: These people really are out for the money. Well, not exactly. They are after the final result of their pursuit, whatever that result might be. Many times it is money, but it could be anything. These people will always pick the easiest path toward the final goal with the least resistance. This differs from the achievement-motivated person who might very well go after the most challenging route to the end result, even if it didn't pay the highest reward.

Security motivation: These folks are more concerned with keeping the status quo than anything else. If they go after a difficult goal, it is because it was their only hope of maintaining their current situation. The will rarely throw caution to the wind to achieve something new. Their main focus is on not losing things. They don't like risk. Great rewards don't motivate them much if there is even a moderate risk involved. Oftentimes, these people are very competent at what they do. They got that way because they selected something to go after that they knew they could master pretty easily. Once it was mastered, they stayed right there. They didn't want to climb the achievement ladder any further because they didn't want to risk what they had already gained.

Power motivation: These people will always be looking for the big hit. They can be achievers to a degree, but often they will go into ventures where there is a very great risk versus reward. They figure that if they hit it big, they can claim that it was all their intellect that got them there. If they don't, they can claim that it was just bad luck. Either way, they will continue to swing for the fences until they either hit it big or strike out so badly that they are forced into a lower standard of life. They will still have dreams and aspirations of becoming the big shot even if they are at a lower station of life than they like. For some reason, these people want to be seen to be powerful and successful. Their surface motivators are usually materialistic things, like cars or fancy houses. These are not true motivators, though. The need to be seen as powerful is always lying beneath the surface. There is some underlying reason for this, but like I said, I'm not a psychologist.

Core Beliefs

Figuring out the motivator for you is just one piece of the puzzle. You have to sit down and figure out what it is that really makes you tick. You have to get past all the surface beliefs of what you think would make you happy and get down to the nitty gritty. For example, a lot of people would say that they want to achieve a goal to get a lot of money. What is money anyway? It is just a piece of paper with some writing on it. In today's fiat currency societies, it means less and less. The money is no longer backed by physical gold and silver. No one in their right mind would want that piece of paper. What they are really saying is that they want the things that go with that money. They want the emotions and the experiences that go with the money. They might want the money for security for themselves and their families. They might want the money to buy things to show off to their friends and to brag. They might want the money to accumulate a big number in their bank account because that is something that might make them feel like they have arrived in life. They might want the money to prove to their true love that they are a good enough provider to be a good spouse. They might want the money to travel to an exotic location and experience what they have always heard about. There are as many different emotions and experiences as you can imagine. The possibilities are endless. One thing is for sure: nobody wants that stupid little piece of paper with the writing on it.

If you can find a couple of hours to sit quietly and be really honest with yourself, you should be able to come up with your own personal core belief system. This can only be found when you can force yourself to tear down the façade of materialistic stuff that everyone says you need to have to be successful. You also have to figure out your private motivator that overrides all others. You need to know what will give you the greatest power over temptation so you can motivate yourself when you need it most.

Enthusiasm

No chapter on motivation would be conclusive without at least some discussion on enthusiasm. If motivation is the fuel that drives the whole system, then surely enthusiasm is the additive to the fuel that makes it run smoothly and provides that little punch. Enthusiasm for any project gives it energy. Enthusiasm gives it excitement. Enthusiasm is the close relative to optimism. When times are looking tough in any situation, inner enthusiasm can halt the decline of the process until the proper motivation can be found. When times are going well, enthusiasm can give you extra mileage on the same tank of gas. Sometimes you just need the little extra push you get from this magical substance.

Earlier, we stated that the Law of Motivation was placed in the number eleven spot for a reason. It is useful in other places in the sequence, but it is not as necessary in the beginning. The reason is that enthusiasm is triggered in its greatest quantity when we first have our a-ha moment. The enthusiasm carries over to the formation of the ideal goal. Enthusiasm gives us plenty of juice in the beginning and doesn't really start to wane until we hit the tough segment of action laws. Even then, it allows us to give more effort than would otherwise be possible.

When I was building my solo dental practice back in the last century, I had a few good, honest motives, but I didn't need to define them to provide the proper motivation for a long time. It was the enthusiasm that carried me during the first few laws of the sequence toward the goal of building my own dental practice. As I was picking out the land on which to build and drawing up plans, I was still tingling with the excitement of the prospect of my own shop. As I was hiring a carpenter, I was still plenty enthused. While I worked fourteen-hour manual labor days until the office was ready to open, I was carried primarily on the enthusiasm that was created the day I made my final decision to go for it. It was not until much later on in the process that I needed to call on true motivation to help me keep my discipline up.

P.P.S.

Perfectly Precise Summary

1.) This law can be used to aid in the advancement through any other law, and should be.

2.) You must define your core beliefs about yourself, honestly and thoroughly.

3.) Find out what your true motivators are and use them to achieve your goal.

4.) Find creative ways to use enthusiasm to get through the tough patches.

Chapter 12

Law 12: The Golden Rule
All Hail the King

From ancient times until now, the rulers of the day have been the ones with the riches. These riches could be gold, jewels, technology, or whatever was most valuable. The truth is that these riches were not the true currency the people were trading. All the things mentioned above were simply manifestations of the one true currency that has existed on the world since the dawn of the ages. I am talking about the precious commodity of time. Time exists in the same measure for all of us, individually. When the Egyptian pharaohs built the pyramids, they were really rich in their commandment of other people's time. When steamboats and railroads were introduced into the world, their creators were made rich because they sold time: they had shortened the amount of time it took to move from point A to point B. Bill Gates has become the richest man in the world because he sold us time in the form of software that shortened the lengths to which we must go to move information around. Time has always been the truest currency and the most difficult commodity to harness and build upon. Unless you are in command of a great troop of other people, you only have so much at your disposal. You won't get any more, and you can't lay it up for a rainy day. You must spend it now and spend it wisely. If it is any comfort, time is also the great equalizer; you possess just as much of this treasure as the richest sultan in Arabia. Just don't try to get a banker to give you a loan based on that collateral. They do have rules, you know.

I will make the case here that the richest man on the planet at any given time is the one who best commands the laws of time. I have put this chapter last because although I believe that you could use these laws for ill-gotten gain for a short period of time, ultimately, your kingdom will perish if you don't follow the Golden Rule. That is not to say that the Golden Rule doesn't permeate the entirety of this book; it does. You should apply its principles from the very inception of the ideal goal at the a-ha moment to your true motives in life. If you do this, your freshly polished achievement should stand the test of time.

What is the Golden Rule? A simple definition would be that you should always treat others as you want to be treated yourself. You can dive deeper into this as you like, but it mainly means that you should always give a fair deal to every other being you impact.

The fair deal may not mean all that you think it does. Do you think it is fair to someone else to be so fiercely democratic that you barely test them before you hire them for a certain position? You cannot superficially select people by education, physical appearance, or general demeanor if you want to get this right. You have to look more deeply and find those inner aptitudes and traits of character that have not changed for that person, regardless of outside influences. If you give a person who is achievement-motivated a job where these is plenty of security, but very little chance of advancement, you will surely doom them to a life of languish. They will never be able to bring the spotlight to their abilities the way they would if they worked for some other boss. If you are in a position of hiring, when you see a young applicant, do you try to find out whether or not they are mentally, physically, morally, or industrially ready to make this a life's work? If not, you are doing them a great disservice and robbing them of time that they can no longer use to shine in their particular best setting.

We have already talked about King Leonidas of Sparta in the chapter on the Law of Discipline. His name has thundered down through the ages. When Xerxes and his million men first invaded Greece with an army culled from forty-six nations, he offered Leonidas the chance to be his own warlord king over the newly proposed Persian province. Leonidas spurned the offer and first met Xerxes's army with 8,000 men of varied Greek backgrounds. Nonetheless, when it became obvious that the day would be lost by the treachery of another Greek man, Leonidas refined his troops down to just his 300 men of Sparta and a few Thespians to help out. This select force was completely refined. It was a war machine, and the members of that elite unit knew, expected, and embraced glorious death in battle. Would Leonidas have been using the fair deal if he had let the rest of his 8,000-man band stay to die? No, he needed a very specialized person to help him forward his cause, and the rest were set free to live another day.

There are three qualities you must possess if you are to follow the Golden Rule to the fullest extent. Understand that these three qualities are rarely found in the same person. This is especially true if the person doesn't know about them or that they are important.

Empathy: The fair person must have empathy for all others. They must be able to put themselves in the shoes of the other person and walk a mile. They must then use this quality to make decisions that affect the other person for good, rather than to take advantage. A person who has the true quality of empathy will usually become a success in life if that is the only one of the three qualities they possess.

Imagination: The truly creative person will look at facts and opportunities and see right through them. They will be able to see what these facts will mean to themselves and others down the road. A person with imagination will have the unique ability to build such wonders that all men should benefit from them. You can have imagination and only use it for your own gain, but that would be in direct opposition to the Law of the Golden Rule and that gain will swiftly depart from you.

Justice: Some people have this inner sense of public morality that allows them to clearly divide actions based on what is best for all. This is not as cut and dried as it seems. Many times, the answer is not right in front of your eyes and you must be tremendously perceptive to see the truth. King Solomon comes to mind. He was perhaps the wisest man in history in regards to his sense of justice. However, at the end of his life, he lamented that he had wasted much of his precious time in frivolous pursuits of wealth, money, and experience. It seems that he mastered all these three qualities in regards to other people but did not include himself in the equation. There is a lesson here: a person cannot be just to everyone if they don't think of themselves as part of the equation. Think about how many more people Solomon might have helped had he taken care of himself too.

If you don't have all three of these qualities and you don't think you can learn them right away, there is another way to get the most out of this rule. I would strongly suggest that you study and learn to obtain all these qualities in the greatest quantity you can. You can form an alliance with other people who might possess the quality you lack. Perhaps they also have a deficit in one or two of the qualities and would benefit from a relationship with you. That would be a fair application of the Law of the Golden Rule.

Think of it this way: A truly great storybook is a rarity. People who have created a memorable work in this area have very rarely done all the jobs required to bring the project to life. A great storybook needs a great illustrator, a great storyteller, and a great editor to make the final product shine. It is doubtful that you could find someone who possessed all three skills in the proportions necessary to build a truly great, enduring work. It is the same way with the three qualities of the

Golden Rule. Rarely will you find a person who naturally possesses all these traits. But just as a great illustrator can learn to become a great editor, you can learn the characteristics you lack.

The Story of the Three Women and the Bread

WHO BROUGHT
THE KNIFE?

If you would like a more symbolic example, consider this. Three women come together for the express purpose of baking a loaf of sourdough bread. All three women bring something of benefit to the project. The very empathetic woman brought the dough. This dough was very special because it had been created using the same yeast that had helped the entire village make bread. The second woman, a very creative lass, molded the dough into a beautiful loaf and baked it at just the right temperature. The bread turned out beautifully and they were all very happy. Then, they encountered a problem. All of them deserved an exact third of the finished loaf of bread. Never fear, the last woman brought a very sharp knife. She whipped it out and delicately carved the wondrous loaf of bread into three distinct but exactly proportional pieces. Now, if only the empathetic one had thought to bring something to drink. Still, I think this is a good illustration of the three necessary qualities you need to master this law.

Let me share an excerpt from my newsletter that explains one time that I think I obeyed the Golden Rule pretty well. At the very least, I showed the quality of empathy and it really paid off.

A few years ago, I was lying on my couch after watching the late college football game on ESPN. It was about 11:30 and I was almost nodding off when the phone rang. Everyone else in the house was fast asleep. Usually when the phone rings in the middle of the night, it is bad news. Most times, it is really bad news. I was hesitant to answer the phone. I looked at the caller ID and I didn't recognize the number or the name. I don't always answer in this situation, but I went ahead and picked up the line this time.

One the other end was a husband who was obviously in a bad spot. He introduced himself, but I still didn't know who he was. He said that he had taken his wife to the emergency room for a toothache, but they still couldn't help her and she was in so much pain he didn't know what to do. He said that their normal dentist hadn't returned their calls all weekend and he was desperate to help his wife. I am not saying that I go into the office every time I get one of these calls. I don't. However, something about this call made me decide to go in to try to help.

When I woke up my wife to tell her that I was going into the office, she didn't want me to do it. She always wonders why I have to be the one to help other dentists' patients when they don't respond on the weekends. She also worries about me going in at night by myself. I don't necessarily disagree with her in principle. But there are real humans involved and I try to think about that, too.

Anyway, I went in to the office. When I got there, I found them waiting. I let them in the back door and we went to one of my preset weekend rooms. **This is a good time to point out a very important thing we do to make my life easier. Every week at the end of the work week, I have my assistants set up one room for an exam, one room for a filling or crown, and one room for a root canal.** *This allows me to walk in on the rare occasion and get the job done without running around after all the instruments that I can't find and looking like I don't know what I am doing to the patients.*

I sat her down and see that she is having pain on #19. #19 had been crowned a few months earlier by the patient's dentist. It had been sensitive for a while, but decided to blow up on this particular weekend. An X-ray revealed a big periapical radiolucency on the distal root. I hated the idea of opening up this thing at midnight on a Saturday night by myself, but I didn't see much of an option. I numbed her up, which gave her some relief for once that weekend, and then I placed the rubber dam which was sitting on the template nicely with the clamp already in place. I accessed the tooth and pus came pouring out. I filed it a little bit and made sure all the drainage was done, and then I placed a cotton pellet and temporized over that. The emergency room had already taken care of the antibiotics and pain medicine, so I didn't have to do much else. As you can imagine, they were appreciative. I recommended that they come back the next week and I would finish the root canal and they said they would. I have heard that before. Sometimes when I do something like this, I get a patient out of the deal, sometimes I don't. You can't go around getting your feelings hurt if the person decides to go back to their old dentist.

In this case, however, something amazing happened. They were better than their word. It turned out that the husband owned a business in a nearby town with about forty employees. Not only did they return for the finished root canal and a new crown the next week, but both the husband and wife became great patients. Then all four of their kids and their spouses became patients. All the kids in the family became patients. Many of the employees of the company and their families became patients. Their relatives are all becoming patients. To top it all off, they are from a small town of about 1,000 people about forty-five minutes from Ripley. Their hometown is closer to another town than it is to Ripley that has twice as many people and three times as many dentists as Ripley. Those people traditionally go to the bigger town to the dentist, and always have. When I performed the midnight root canal, I only had a smattering of about twelve patients from this little town. Now I have over a hundred. To me, that is amazing. In essence, I have created a little beachhead there in that little town that naturally shouldn't exist.

All that is to say that you should never underestimate the sheer power that comes from ONE great referrer or from ONE selfless act. Don't go around expecting to get this kind of result from every procedure you do, but eventually, you should get lucky and get one of these things going.

I believe that I was following the Golden Rule here because I was able to understand the pain of the wife. I also felt the pain in the husband's voice because he knew that his wife needed help and he couldn't do anything to help her. I can assure you that I had no deep desire to get out of my house at midnight to go see a patient who wasn't even one of my own. In fact, she had been a patient of my former employer's. I don't know why I didn't just tell her that she would have to wait until he could see her. I could have chosen that path without being in the wrong morally. However, I ultimately chose to help my fellow man in a time of need. Thank goodness I did. Just like I told in the above story, they really have been better than their word in every way.

P.P.S.

Perfectly Precise Summary

1.) The Golden Rule has been in existence forever and has been recorded since biblical times.

2.) We must be fair to ourselves and all others to succeed and maintain our goals.

3.) When in doubt, err in the favor of the other person involved.

4.) What you do for others will always come back to you many times over.

Section III

Workbook

This is where it all comes together. If you have an aversion to physically writing in this book, photocopy this section so you can work through it, make corrections, and chart your goal progress. Don't forget that this is not a one-shot deal. You should use these steps any time you are trying to design, achieve, and implement any worthwhile thing into your life. I truly feel that the time has come for a system like this due to our current society's severe inclination towards hectic and crazy lifestyles. If we are going to find the inner strength to insert anything else into our daily routine or set of personal skills, we need a definitive roadmap to lead the way. This workbook is that roadmap.

****

Pre-goal

_____

_____

Why have you chosen this as your pre-goal?

_____

_____

How do you think you would feel if you accomplished this?

_____

_____

Law 1—Goals

In this exercise, I want you to figure out your true core belief system. You need to sit down in a quiet place and consider what it is that makes you tick. Here is how you do it.

First, name the thing that you want to attain while achieving your goal. (HINT: It is your pre-goal with a little more definition.) If your pre-goal was to lose weight, here you would write something like, "To lose weight and get rock-hard abs."

You may have put down something like *rock-hard abs* or *a new sports car.* That's fine for now. However, you must figure out what really makes you tick. It isn't the stuff we're after; it's the feeling the stuff gives us. If your pre-goal is rock-hard abs, you might really be concerned about things like the lack of embarrassment at the beach, the attention of women, or the pride you feel when you take your shirt off at the gym. You don't really care about the abs; *you care about the way they make you feel.*

Now you have to get more serious about this project and form your Definite Ideal Goal (DIG). It must be very specific and reflect your core belief system. *For example: Definite Ideal Goal: "To work out four days a week for two hours a day, measuring my progress until I have lost fifty pounds and can see obvious definition in my abdominal region from the muscles I have built. I will also use the strategy of eating 1,500 calories per day with a diet very low in white carbohydrates and very high in fiber and green leafy vegetables. I will also hire a personal trainer to make sure that I am following through with my DIG. I will deny myself the new purchase of the sixty-inch plasma screen TV that I want to purchase until this DIG is obtained. When my DIG is obtained, I will take my family on a vacation to Hawaii, where we will play on the beach and I will be proud to take off my shirt. I will feel proud of my figure when my wife smiles at me the way she does when she is flirting. I will continue to work out at the pace prescribed by my personal trainer after the DIG is achieved to maintain my weight and muscle definition."*

Now, that is a Definite Ideal Goal. You write yours below. Use extra paper if you need it, just keep up with it.

_____

_____

_____

_____

Law 2—Right Mind

You must shed your Rate-limiting Factors (RLFs) from your mind if you are to succeed moving forward.

Define three RLFs and then provide the reasons they are false. If they turn out to be true, you need to go back to Law 1 and redo that one.

> Example: Rate-limiting Factor: "I believe I am too old to succeed at this DIG."

> Reason it is false: "I know many other people that are older than I who have accomplished this very same thing. They are Mr. XYZ, etc., etc."

Rate-limiting Factor #1: _____

Reason it is false: _____

Rate-limiting Factor #2: _____

Reason it is false: _____

Rate-limiting Factor #3: _____

Reason it is false: _____

Law 3—Belief

Name five Inspirational things you can do to help get your mind in the right place to believe in yourself. If you finished the Law of the Right Mind correctly, then it can only be you standing in the way of your success. The five things I would do if I needed a boost of motivation would be to watch *Rocky, Hoosiers,* and *The Natural.* Then I would listen to my motivational remix on my MP3 player. Last, I would read my favorite quotes from the Bible.

Resource: Nowadays, you can go to YouTube and watch your favorite clips from all your favorite movies. This saves the time of watching the whole thing and it gives me the same feeling as watching the whole movie. Just go to *www.youtube.com.*

Inspirational Immersion Exercise

What five things will you do to inspire yourself?

Action #1 _____

Action #2 _____

Action #3 _____

Action #4 _____

Action #5 _____

Law 4—Courage

In this exercise, I want you to write down at least three examples of each fear you will likely face as you go forward in the implementation of your goal. Then, write down three ways you will overcome these fears in the spaces below each example. This will give you tremendous strength as you actually face these fears later on. You will have already imagined them and how they will make you feel. You will also have thought about how you will handle them. This should give you the strength to push on to the next Law.

FEAR OF FAILURE #1 Example _____

    #1 Strategy to overcome _____

    #2 Strategy to overcome _____

    #3 Strategy to overcome _____

FEAR OF REJECTION #1 Example _____

    #1 Strategy to overcome _____

    #2 Strategy to overcome _____

    #3 Strategy to overcome _____

FEAR OF LOSS #1 Example _____

    #1 Strategy to overcome _____

    #2 Strategy to overcome _____

    #3 Strategy to overcome _____

Law 5—Visual Learning

First, you must think of three good examples of people who have seen succeed in your DIG. There will be many, but pick the three you admire the most.

Then, pick only one of them to try to really study. Maybe you can even watch one of them performing their skill in person. If not, hopefully they will have study resources that you can purchase or acquire to really understand the way they accomplished their skill. Really dig in and spend a lot of time researching this one person. Of course, if your first choice turns out to be a real jerk or if there isn't much way to get study materials from them, go to the second person on your list. You get bonus points for studying all three people on your list.

Name three people who have had success in the field of your DIG. Rank them in your own personal order of merit.

#1 _____

#2 _____

#3 _____

Now, choose one name to research, study, and possibly personally model by visual learning.

Law 6—Operations

This exercise is the first one to require you to get off your tail and really do something. You can't talk about a project forever. You have to finally start it.

To know how you are doing, you have to keep some records. We are going to start a statistics binder. You have to learn the value and the simple magic of measurement. Anything that is measured will grow. In this case, it will be the growth of your progress in pursuit of your DIG.

In this exercise, I want you to choose five things that would be of value to measure as you work your way through the cycle of time laws. For example: If your DIG is the one about the abs, etc., your five statistics might be:

1.) Weight by week

2.) Body fat by week

3.) Max sit-ups by week

4.) Max pull-ups by week

5.) Max push-ups by week

One of the graphs would look something like this:

Statistic 1

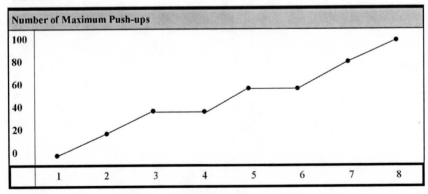

Week Number

You would keep these stats posted where you could see them for the duration of this particular DIG. If things draw out longer than you thought, you can change the dimensions of the x or y axis and make them into monthly or yearly as need be. The point is that you must physically chart your progress. There is something about measuring yourself that will force you to try harder to achieve.

You own personal five statistics to keep:

#1 _____

#2 _____

#3 _____

#4 _____

#5 _____

Law 7—Logistics

Now that you have started to actually do something, you have surely run into some challenges. Let's call them roadblocks. To get around these roadblocks, you will need some detailed descriptions of the roadblocks themselves. Then you need to come up with three possible solutions around them. Don't worry if you have one so insurmountable that you have to go back a couple of laws and redirect your efforts. This is part of everyone faces that's same issue at some point. Let's work through them.

Roadblock #1_____

    Possible solution #1_____

    Possible solution #2_____

    Possible solution #3_____

Roadblock #2_____

    Possible solution #1_____

    Possible solution #2_____

    Possible solution #3_____

Roadblock #3_____

    Possible solution #1_____

    Possible solution #2_____

    Possible solution #3_____

Now that you've cleared the path of obstructions, you should have laid the groundwork for good, smooth schedules within your DIG and the path to achievement and implementation of that goal.

Next, what are some tools that you could place into your life or business that would make it easier? Think about the story of the route board from my own dental practice. What could you implement into your situation that would make the goal easier to obtain and retain?

Idea #1 _____

_____

Idea #2 _____

_____

Idea #3 _____

_____

Law 8—Environment

Now that things are working pretty well, you may have even already achieved your DIG. You need to make your life a little easier and set the stage for retaining your achievement.

Name three things that you could do for yourself that would make the retention of your DIG easier.

Example: If I had designed a new way of keeping track of my projects and succeeded at that DIG, I would probably want to move on to another goal or project. Maybe three good ways to help my environment to make retention easier would be:

1.) *Give my personal assistant the order to check up on the system once a week and report back to me.*
2.) *Train the manager of that particular area in the new system.*
3.) *Give an incentive to that manager if the new system is implemented by a certain date.*

That would be very specific and keep the chances of the new system retention very high.

Three Retention Strategies

Strategy #1 _____

_____

Strategy #2 _____

_____

Strategy #3 _____

_____

Law 9—Standard Operating Procedures

Now you get to build your own SOP for your Definite Ideal Goal (DIG). (You need to go back to the chapter on SOPs and look at the list of topic areas for this.) Then you can go down the list and define each area as much as you need. You don't absolutely have to use every topic listed in the chapter, but that would make it just that much more clear and definitive.

Go down and write a simple description of each of the topics listed below. Then you can type out a several-page SOP and expand on each topic. Do this first, and then I'll tell you what to do with it. Refer back to the descriptions of each topic in the chapter.

1.) **Purpose**
2.) **Scope**
3.) **Definitions**
4.) **Description**
5.) **Training**
6.) **Personnel involved**
7.) **Procedure**
8.) **Equipment**
9.) **Precautions**
10.) **Reference**

Now that you have a short description of each of these, you can write your real SOP. Just take each topic and go into great detail about every little aspect of the DIG you have just achieved. You have already done some of this work. When we developed our detailed DIG back in Law 1, we gave a very detailed purpose for wanting to do the DIG in the first place. You can modify that one and add to it, but that should pretty much cover the purpose topic. You just go down the line and give all the reasons and details for each topic. It will take a couple of hours to get it perfect, but then you will really have something. You can add this

SOP into a manual of SOPs that contain all the SOPs of all the DIGs you have accomplished. Now, you have a very detailed description of your success that is reproducible. Theoretically, you could hand this off to someone else with no experience in the area and they could achieve this particular goal. That comes in handy in a company or organization. It will also come in handy for you. Even after you have succeeded, you will occasionally need to remember what got you to this point in life. You may even occasionally need to update the SOP. No problem; that's what it is there for. This manual will become a treasured belonging of yours forever.

Law 10—Discipline

Here we want to define our own weaknesses that may give us trouble as we try to maintain our success. Look deep inside and be honest about our potential pitfalls. Then we want to give each weakness three ways that we will persevere through them. After that we want to give three ways that we will focus on maintaining our goal in the face of that weakness. This exercise will make us stronger and define our true enemies of progress.

Weakness #1_____

    Perseverance method #1_____

_____

Focus in the face of weakness_____

_____

Weakness #2_____

    Perseverance method #1_____

_____

Focus in the face of weakness_____

_____

Weakness #3_____

    Perseverance method #1_____

_____

Focus in the face of weakness_____

Law 11—Motivation

We will go back to the core belief concept. To truly discover the motivation that drives us forward and propels us to keep going even in the face of adversity, we must know ourselves. Answer a few questions about your true thoughts, and then we will give ourselves great power with an exercise. Be honest.

Question #1: If you had the choice of fame or money, which would you choose?

Question #2: If you had the choice of recognition or results, which would you choose?

Question #3: If you could only live one day for the rest of your life and not get tired of it, what would that day look like? Describe in detail. Include your feelings and thoughts about the day's events. Be sure to include your answers to questions 2 and 3 into this perfect day.

_____

_____

_____

_____

_____

Now, there are no wrong answers here. Hopefully you were honest with yourself. Remember, you can use another sheet of paper to write these things out if you don't want others to see them.

The exercise

Define five ways that you will try to utilize the achievement and implementation of the DIG to move toward your answer to question #3.

Utilization #1

_____

_____

Utilization #2

_____

_____

Utilization #3

_____

_____

Utilization #4

_____

_____

Utilization #5

_____

_____

Law 12—The Golden Rule

Now we're almost done. I told you in the last chapter of the book about how important it is to use these laws for good instead of evil. Now, you must write down five ways that you know the achievement of this DIG will help other people and make the world a better place. One example of this with the DIG of the rock-hard abs DIG from the first example would be this:

The world is a better place because:

1.) *I am now more confident and I treat people more kindly every day.*
2.) *I now have the confidence to talk more freely to people. This has allowed me to start my own company and hire four people. Their families benefit from their salaries.*
3.) *I am healthier and I can teach my kids how to be healthier.*
4.) *I have better self-confidence and that has made my marriage better. Now my kids will see a good marriage to give them better visual learning on that subject.*
5.) *I have become a better role model to other people who are struggling to stay in shape. They can model me and get healthier themselves.*

#1. The world is a better place because

_____

_____

_____

#2. The world is a better place because

_____

_____

_____

#3. The world is a better place because

_____

_____

_____

#4. The world is a better place because

_____

_____

_____

#5. The world is a better place because

_____

_____

_____

There you have it. You have successfully completed this workbook and the DIG you started out the book with. You can file away a copy of this workbook section with your SOPs as an attachment to the reference section and you are done. It is either time to take a little break from the success track, or if you have developed an addiction to achieving goals, pick out another one and let's get going. It will be easier the second time around.

A-ha Moments

#1.

_____

_____

_____

_____

#2.

_____

_____

_____

_____

#3.

_____

_____

_____

_____

#4.

_____

_____

_____

_____

#5.

_____

_____

_____

_____

#6.

_____

_____

_____

_____

#7.

_____

_____

_____

_____

About the Author

Why should you listen to Chris Griffin? After all, he admits to being lazy for most of his life.

He did have a few good accomplishments early on. He was a Valedictorian in high school and he became a doctor at age 24 after finishing dental school. These accomplishments were <u>commendable</u>, but not all that uncommon. The real evidence of his organizational talents surfaced after he faced a crossroads in his life.

On July 1st, 1999, Dr. Griffin found himself with no job, no prospects, and a wife expecting their first child. Something changed that day. Dr. Griffin was forced to put aside all excuses and face the reality that he hadn't lived up to his potential. Dr. Griffin dug in his heels and decided to build his own dental practice in his hometown. After purchasing an old house and starting from zero, Dr. Griffin was able to squeeze all the steps of building, renovating, purchasing, and organizing into an incredible timeframe. On August 30th, 2009, the doors were opened at the Griffin Dental Group and the first patient was treated. During that process Dr. Griffin discovered that just about any goal, however daunting, could be achieved using the proper sequence of actions.

During his professional career, Dr. Griffin has attacked the industry norms and implemented systems into his practice that streamlined procedures over and over again. At age 29 Dr. Griffin became the youngest person ever to receive a Fellowship from the Academy of General Dentistry from the state of Mississippi. Very few people have ever received that award before age 30 due to the demanding schedule required. Eventually, Dr. Griffin began teaching his concepts and systems to dentists all over North America through his company, Capacity College.

Time Genius came about as an outgrowth of the systems that Dr. Griffin teaches his students to better help them achieve their goals and implement systems into their practices. Dr. Griffin truly believes that any person can succeed if they only know where to start and what system to follow. Time Genius provides the framework that guides achievement and implementation.

Free Bonus Gift

Your *FREE* Bonus worth $297.00: Instant Download!

Thank you for your investment in "Time Genius". As an added bonus only for our readers and for a very limited time we are offering you our "Mind Mapping Time and Goals Program".

Congratulations! When you bought this book, you also qualified for this special FREE BONUS PROGRAM worth $297.00. We are only offering this to our readers and for a very limited time.

This program is training on how to incorporate the use of mindmaps into your life and business. I still remember the day and place where I first heard about mind maps. Their incorporation into my own life changed things forever. Mind maps gave me the ability to organize thoughts, ideas, and goals rapidly. That speed was translated into everything and finally resulted in the creation of Time Genius.

In the Mind Mapping Time and Goals Program you will instantly get:

- A Mind Mapping Video Tutorial with transcript

- Our Report: "Using Mind Maps to Bend Time and Achieve Goals"

- Case Study Reviews on Mind Maps

- PLUS a mystery audio bonus that will speed up implementation of the program.

Visit the Website Below to Download Your FREE BONUS now before time is up!

www.timegeniusbook.com/bonus

BUY A SHARE OF THE FUTURE IN YOUR COMMUNITY

These certificates make great holiday, graduation and birthday gifts that can be personalized with the recipient's name. The cost of one S.H.A.R.E. or one square foot is $54.17. The personalized certificate is suitable for framing and will state the number of shares purchased and the amount of each share, as well as the recipient's name. The home that you participate in "building" will last for many years and will continue to grow in value.

Here is a sample SHARE certificate:

YES, I WOULD LIKE TO HELP!

I support the work that Habitat for Humanity does and I want to be part of the excitement! As a donor, I will receive periodic updates on your construction activities but, more importantly, I know my gift will help a family in our community realize the dream of homeownership. **I would like to SHARE in your efforts against substandard housing in my community!** *(Please print below)*

PLEASE SEND ME _____ SHARES at $54.17 EACH = $ $_____

In Honor Of: _____

Occasion: (Circle One)   HOLIDAY   BIRTHDAY   ANNIVERSARY

      OTHER: _____

Address of Recipient: _____

Gift From: _____ *Donor Address:* _____

Donor Email: _____

I AM ENCLOSING A CHECK FOR $ $_____ PAYABLE TO HABITAT FOR HUMANITY OR PLEASE CHARGE MY VISA OR MASTERCARD *(CIRCLE ONE)*

Card Number _____ Expiration Date: _____

Name as it appears on Credit Card _____ Charge Amount $ _____

Signature _____

Billing Address _____

Telephone # Day _____ Eve _____

PLEASE NOTE: Your contribution is tax-deductible to the fullest extent allowed by law.
Habitat for Humanity • P.O. Box 1443 • Newport News, VA 23601 • 757-596-5553
www.HelpHabitatforHumanity.org

LaVergne, TN USA
09 September 2010
196425LV00006B/1/P